ESSAYS ON POETRY BY *John Stuart Mill*

# ESSAYS ON POETRY

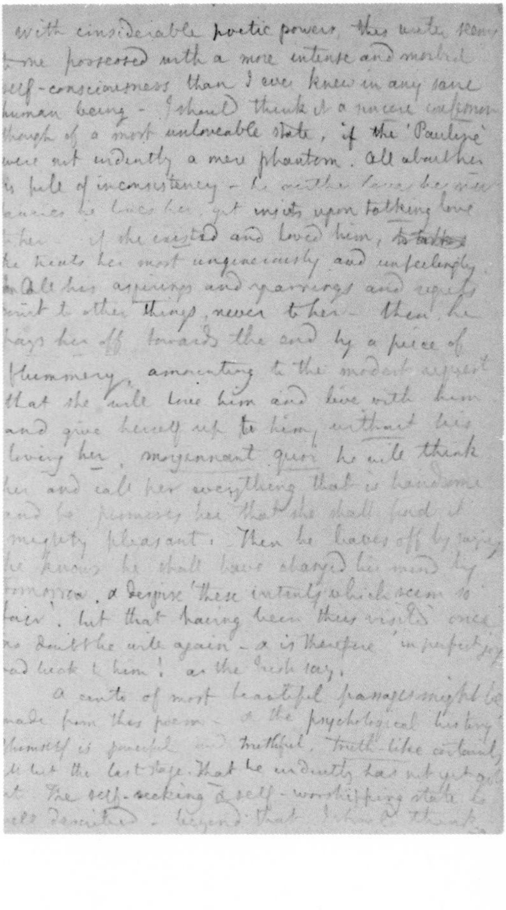

Y *John Stuart Mill*

Edited by
F. Parvin Sharpless

UNIVERSITY OF SOUTH CAROLINA PRESS

COLUMBIA, SOUTH CAROLINA

LIBRARY OF CONGRESS CATALOGING IN PUBLICATION DATA
Mill, John Stuart, 1806–1873.
  Essays on poetry.

  Bibliography: p.
  Includes index.
  1.   Poetry—History and criticism—Addresses,
essays, lectures.   I.   Title.
PN1136.M5   1976      809.1      76–40162
ISBN 0–87249–341–5

# Contents

# Introduction

IT MAY BE that the idea of John Stuart Mill as a literary critic, as a reader and reviewer of poetry, as a formulator of poetics is so startling as to bring to mind Dr. Johnson's familiar comment upon a woman preaching a sermon: "It is not done well; but you are surprized to find it done at all." If so, it is because we have been too much influenced by an image of Mill that is only half true: Mill as a man of icy and controlled manners, of stern, even prudish morality, of stiff and forbidding appearance, and with a mind so devoted to logic as to make logical errors in its defense. Mill, we are told, lacked all normal human feeling; he had no warmth, no heart. From Carlyle's remark in 1831 that his new acquaintance may "come to something; yet to nothing poetical I think: his fancy is not rich; furthermore, he cannot laugh with any compass,"[1] to Ruskin's conclusion in 1877 that "John Stewart [sic] Mill had no more sap in him than a toothpick, and no more fancy than a toadstool,"[2] Mill has been seen as a mechanical man, unlikely ever to have read poetry, let alone to be able to write about it.

There is, however, another side of Mill's personality, which the *Autobiography* and these remarks conceal. From the let-

[1] James Anthony Froude, *Thomas Carlyle* (New York, 1882), II: 162.
[2] John Ruskin, *The Diaries of John Ruskin*, ed. Joan Evans and John Howard Whitemore (Oxford, 1959), January 16, 1877.

ters, from his diary, from the testimony of those who under-
stood him better than Carlyle, comes a different picture, one
that gives proper weight to his "poetic" side. Mill's friend and
first biographer Alexander Bain noted that Mill possessed con-
siderable "tender feelings,"[3] and John Sterling referred to Mill's
"warm, upright and really lofty soul."[4] To some, indeed, this
part of Mill's personality seemed stronger than it should be.
Charles Eliot Norton observed in 1870 that Mill's intense devo-
tion to the cause of women's rights "has a tendency to develop
the sentimental part of his intelligence, which is of immense
force, and has only been kept in due subjection by his respect
for his own reason."[5] The fact is that Mill had a great deal of
feeling and a quite poetic sensibility, but with the exception of
his devotion to Harriet Taylor, these qualities were almost en-
tirely attached to abstract philosophic principles. These prin-
ciples, however, were never given validity by the feeling toward
them; only reason, following empirical procedures, could do
that. To put it another way, Mill frequently loved what his
reason held to be true, but truth was not established by love.
Often this feeling shines through the rational texture of his
philosophic writing, and when it does, we have his most
eloquent and striking work: *On Liberty, Utilitarianism, Three
Essays on Religion*, and the *St. Andrew's Inaugural Address*.
Poetry, then, that expressed a similar feeling for acceptable
truths was sure to move him.[6] He was, as he said of himself,
"capable of almost any degree of *exalté* feeling from poetry,"[7]

[3] Alexander Bain, *John Stuart Mill* (London, 1882), p. 150.
[4] Anne Kimball Tuell, *John Sterling* (New York, 1941), p. 69.
[5] Charles Eliot Norton, *Letters of Charles Eliot Norton*, ed. Sara Norton and
M. A. DeWolfe Howe (Boston, 1913), I: 400.
[6] See Bertrand and Patricia Russell, *The Amberley Papers, the Letters and Diaries
of Bertrand Russell's Parents* (New York, 1937), II: 375: "After dinner Mr. Mill read us
Shelley's Ode to Liberty & he got quite excited & moved over it rocking backwards &
forwards & nearly choking with emotion; he said himself: 'it is almost too much for
one.'"
[7] John Stuart Mill, *The Earlier Letters of John Stuart Mill* (Vols. XII and XIII in
*Collected Works of John Stuart Mill*), ed. Francis E. Mineka (Toronto, 1963), p. 557.

and so long as the poetry was that which recommended individualism, utilitarian morality, cultivation of the mind—in short, as long as the poetry was Philosophic Radical poetry and not Tory poetry—there is no reason to doubt Mill's contention.

But this quality of Mill's personality, though it might have led him to read poetry, would not have produced the criticism and literary theory to be found in these essays and reviews. *They* arise from Mill's growing awareness after 1826 of the inadequacies of the rigid empiricism of the educational practice to which Mill was subjected at the hands of his father and Jeremy Bentham, and the equally rigid epistemological theory on which it was based. Mill's well-known account of this period in his life, found in the *Autobiography* under the heading "A Crisis in my Mental History,"[8] emphasizes the ennui and despair that Mill experienced beginning in the fall of 1826 and treats literature and poetry, Marmontel and Wordsworth, as a kind of psychotherapy. Yet even as one admits the difficulty of disentangling the rational from the irrational, the conscious from the unconscious, a careful reading of the *Autobiography* indicates what these reviews and essays further verify: that much of the difficulty of these years stemmed from intellectual dismay at the possibility of finding the entire basis of his intellectual life false. These essays thus provide one of the best sources for study of the resolution of the "mental crisis," and of the intellectual changes that grew from it, changes that were radical to Mill's entire career. The critical theory evolved is Mill's first attempt to resolve the intellectual problems raised by the crisis and to assimilate within a rational framework what had happened to him.

Mill's account is familiar: in the autumn of 1826, at the age of 20, he finds himself in "a dull state of nerves" caused, he realizes, by the loss of "joy and happiness" that had always be-

---

[8] John Stuart Mill, *Autobiography of John Stuart Mill* (New York, 1924), pp. 93–128.

fore accompanied the thought of the accomplishment of the social and moral reforms so confidently proposed by the utilitarian program of Bentham and James Mill. The realization brings despair: "All my happiness was to have been found in the continual pursuit of this end. The end had ceased to charm, and how could there ever again be any interest in the means? I seemed to have nothing left to live for."[9]

The associationalist psychology upon which the utilitarians based their social programs provided Mill with an explanation of his difficulty. It held that since the mind is a blank slate, any idea could be linked by association with any other idea and also that any idea or sequence of ideas could be associated with either pleasurable or painful feelings. From these premises came the utilitarian hope to employ education to improve men, reform social institutions, and encourage the greatest good for the greatest number. This could be done, they thought, by forming in the minds of as many men as possible an indissoluble link between the feeling of individual pleasure and the idea of the general social good. If in the experience of the individual these two things were linked often enough, and if the feeling involved were of sufficient strength, then the individual would acquire a fixed and automatic associative sequence, and would respond to every moral choice in terms that considered the general social welfare.

Because the corrupt state of society often contaminated men to the extent that no unprejudiced demonstration of this theory was possible, Bentham and James Mill had resolved to apply these principles with the greatest possible rigor to the education of James Mill's eldest son. But in looking back upon the experience, John Mill perceived one difficulty his teachers had overlooked. According to the theory there are two kinds of associative sequences: those based upon "permanent sequences in nature," which—because they are "natural," fixed, and

[9] Mill, *Autobiography*, p. 94.

permanent—become stronger the more they are subjected to rational analysis, and those sequences that are artificial, unnatural, and that, if they are to be permanent, require the reinforcement of associated feelings. These two methods of reinforcement—analysis and feelings—are, however, not always compatible, for when analysis is turned on sequences that are not "natural," it tends to destroy them by showing them to be indeed artificial. Among these artificial sequences was the very one which had provided the motivation for all Mill's actions: the feeling of pleasure that was linked to the achievement of the greatest good for the greatest number. Thus, Mill's difficulty:

> My education, I thought, had failed to create these feelings in sufficient strength to resist the dissolving influence of analysis, while the whole course of my intellectual cultivation had made precocious and premature analysis the inveterate habit of my mind. I was thus, as I said to myself, left stranded at the commencement of my voyage, with a well-equipped ship and a rudder, but no sail; without any real desire for the ends which I had been so carefully fitted out to work for: no delight in virtue, or the general good, but also just as little in anything else.[10]

But this conclusion was based on analysis and, while true, could give Mill little consolation. To realize that one needs feelings is not to achieve them. Thus the vivid sympathy with Marmontel is of great importance because it was a spontaneous, irrational response and demonstrated that his ability to feel had not been totally effaced by his education, that he could yet have feelings and that they could be used to cement the proper ideas together and to reinstate the motive energy towards the social goals of the utilitarian movement.

Consequently, Mill says, though he did not reject his earlier conviction that intellectual and analytic powers were of the

[10] Ibid., pp. 97–98.

highest value, he did begin to attach increased importance to "the internal culture of the individual"; and "the cultivation of the feelings became one of the cardinal points in my ethical and philosophical creed."[11] The experience with Marmontel and later with Wordsworth pointed to literature as the primary source of stimulation for the feelings. "I now began to find meaning in the things which I had read or heard about the importance of poetry and art as instruments of human culture."[12] Wordsworth's poems, read in 1828, provided the "precise thing for my mental wants at that particular juncture": "states of feeling, and of thought coloured by feeling," and as Mill came under the influence of these poems, he felt himself "at once better and happier."[13]

But Mill's account is not fully satisfactory. It suggests only that Mill fell into ennui, he read Wordsworth, his ennui vanished, and he concluded that poetry is a good remedy for low spirits. Part of the difficulty is that the psychological events of the crisis are thought of and described in the limited metaphors of Hartleian theory. Ideas are conceived as particles in the mechanistic universe of the mind, and feeling is a kind of electrical, gravitational glue that magnetizes the ideas into appropriate constellations, giving them at the same time a force and coherence. But a larger part of our difficulty with Mill's account of the crisis is that, despite the implication of the *Autobiography* to the contrary, Mill's crisis raises doubts against the basic premises of Benthamism. These doubts are intellectual not psychological and cannot therefore be removed by an infusion of poetic feeling. Poetry gave Mill a new *modus operandi*, but did not explain why one was required.

In the first place, the mental crisis did occur, and this even-

---

[11]  Ibid., p. 101.
[12]  Ibid., p. 101.
[13]  Ibid., pp. 103–4.

tuality was neither considered nor explainable under utilitarian psychology. A person who has been the recipient of the perfect educational experience should not have mental crises. If he does, something is wrong with the education and with the theory that supports it. Furthermore, if feeling is a necessary antidote to reason, the absolute disdain held by Bentham and James Mill towards it was another error, and a basic one at that. Finally, the crisis suggested that what reason discovers, though it may be true, is not always beneficial to the discoverer. By analytic reason Mill discovered that his motivation for social reform and the moral improvement and happiness of humanity was artificial and subjective, and this truth produced despair and ennui.

"Cultivation of the feelings" was, on intellectual grounds, no solution whatsoever. Before the crisis Mill had accepted the Benthamite view that feelings were at best worthless, at worst dangerous. They could be easily feigned, usually by fops and gentlemen, who, from their fastidious refinement, patronized the lower classes and opposed all social reform. Moreover, feeling was an unreasonable quantity. It allowed the mind to hold to opinions that were false and yet untouchable by rational argument. To rely upon feelings in an intellectual question was no better than to rely upon intuitive judgments, upon *a priori* reasoning; it was to accept the epistemology of what Mill called the "intuitional" school, a school that contained all the enemies of the utilitarian movement: the church, Tories, Carlyleans, Coleridgeans, aristocrats of all kinds, seers, sages, and poets—all men who "knew" truths by intuition, by natural law, or by inherent sensibility, and whose claims were by definition unchallengable by men of reason.

The mental crisis, then, is a Victorian dark night of the soul with the usual values reversed: the citadel of reason and science finding itself undermined and subverted by faith and feeling. From it, Mill learned the lesson of openmindedness, of the many-sidedness of truth; he became the most tolerant of philosophers. But he never compromised his absolute rejection of intuitional metaphysics. While he admitted the value of what he called the Germano-Coleridgean reaction to the eighteenth century, while he readily acknowledged the shortcomings of Benthamism, while he admired Coleridge for his expression of a necessary antithetical intellectual position, the first principle of his metaphysics remained steadfastly experientialist.

> We see no ground for believing that any thing can be the object of our knowledge except our experience, and what can be inferred from our experience by the analogies of experience itself; nor that there is any idea, feeling, or power, in the human mind, which, in order to account for it, requires that its origin should be referred to any other source. [14]

Thus poetry and the feelings it produces must be explained in these terms. After poetry had solved the psychological difficulties, Mill undertakes in the two essays on poetry, the reviews of Tennyson and de Vigny, to solve the intellectual difficulties that poetry raises. In these essays Mill attempts to establish a set of poetics based upon reason and empirical procedure. The poet must be incorporated within the experientialist system; feelings must be reconciled with reason; poetry must be "explained."

"What is Poetry?" begins by affirming Wordsworth's dictum that the opposite of poetry is not prose but science. Each has its own particular kind of truth: the scientific one based upon empirical observation of the external world, the poetic one derived from the inner truth of the feelings. The poet is not interested in the facts and things of the external world for themselves; instead he studies the inner feelings that external objects stimulate in the mind. By presenting only internal feelings the poet reflects a subjective truth, distinct from scientific truth,

[14] John Stuart Mill, "Coleridge," in *Dissertations and Discussions: Political, Philosophical, and Historical* (Boston, 1865), II: 21 (First published by John W. Parker: London, 1859).

*xiv*

one that neither contradicts nor is judged by any reference to the external world. The internal psychological world of poetry and the external empirical world of science are absolutely separated from one another, and the integrity of each within its own sphere is preserved.

Mill goes on to make a distinction between poetry and "eloquence" that has the effect of further isolating the poet. The poet's words are spoken spontaneously, without calculation; they are written to relieve the feelings, with no "lookings-forth into the outward and every-day world." To consider an audience is to lapse from poetry into eloquence. The poet's words are pure of any conscious intention; they are natural and honest; they are, as it were, soliloquized; and a reader of them may be said only to "overhear" a poem. The poet neither writes of the facts of the external world nor does he, consciously at least, write for men living in that world.

In the second essay, "The Two Kinds of Poetry," Mill rejects the idea of the "born" poet, whose unique "gifts" make him a seer, someone possessing by nature intuitive knowledge. The fact that some people write poetry and others do not is not the result of any special vision or ability. If, says Mill, the doctrine of *nascitur poeta* suggests that "any natural peculiarity whatever is implied in producing poetry," the doctrine is false. "Nevertheless, it seems undeniable in point of fact and consistent with the principles of a sound metaphysics, that there are poetic natures." The sound metaphysics are, of course, those of the experientialist school, and Mill thus concludes that the poet differs from ordinary men, not in respect to knowing different truths, not in kind, but only in the degree to which his habitual method of associating ideas is governed by emotional quantities rather than the chronological or sequential categories of experience, or the abstract categories of education.

Shelley is the best example of such a poet, a "Poet of Nature" whose habitual method of association is by means of the feelings attached to ideas rather than by the ideas themselves. But though nature provides feelings, it cannot be allowed to be the source of ideas. Therefore Mill establishes what is a central concept in his critical position, the idea of the logician-poet, or as he later modified the phrase, the philosopher-poet. The philosopher-poet is naturally endowed with emotional sensibility but is equipped also—by study and intellectual discipline —with strong rational faculties. Poetic susceptibility need not, as the older utilitarians had held, inevitably overrule the reason. Reason and feeling, poetry and truth are compatible. By use of the intellect the poet acquires appropriate social and moral ideas, just as a utilitarian philosopher might. But the peculiar susceptibility of the philosopher-poet allows the ideas to become infused with emotion; thus they become more meaningful and alive and are represented in this way in poetry. Moreover, the poetry itself can be of great value to the reformer because it changes philosophic abstractions to felt ideas and makes them capable of moving men to love truth with their hearts *and* know it with their heads.

For Mill no poet ever quite achieved the position of the philosopher-poet. Wordsworth, Mill thought, lacked the emotional sensibility; Shelley died before his intellect could properly develop. Tennyson interested Mill in 1835 because his second volume gave indication of a developing intellectual capacity. Mill admired de Vigny because he wrote poetry and fiction based upon autobiographical fact or historical event, and thus had at hand a body of "truth," though of a lower order than the speculative inquiries of the philosopher. Once formulated, Mill's position on the nature of the poet remained constant. In 1854 he again asserted the poet's function: "The Artist is not the Seer: not he who can detect truth, but he who can clothe a given truth in the most expressive and impressive symbols."[15]

[15] John Stuart Mill, *The Letters of John Stuart Mill*, ed. Hugh S. R. Elliot (London, 1910), II: 386.

*xvi*

In view of the traditional idea of Mill's unyielding rationalism it is perhaps strange to note that the changes that Mill's thinking undergoes during the period between 1826 and 1833 provide an accurate paradigm of that movement in intellectual history usually called the romantic revolt. In the mental crisis and in the responses to it contained in these essays is chronicled a rejection of the naive optimism and simple rationalism of the eighteenth century, especially its inadequate comprehension of the complexity of human personality. In these essays the poet is freed from the restraints of imitative art and is given liberty to express his subjective feelings. Here poetry becomes of value for its content. Here, finally, is literature considered, not by systems of rules, genres, kinds, but as an object of practical value, for achieving psychological health (as in his own case) and for clothing the truths of philosophy in affective terms so they may aid in the struggle for social reform and moral progress.

If this youthful revolt is essentially romantic, Mill's mature view (not fully represented by these essays) is Victorian. With Tennyson, for example, Mill shares a willingness to accept the truths of science even when their consequences are painful, maintaining at the same time what the Victorians called faith, and Mill feeling. With Dickens and George Eliot, Mill shares the view that reason alone cannot support moral value, that morality without sympathy is barren and even impossible. With Arnold, Mill asserts the value of literature as a pragmatic aid in cultivating the mind and raising the moral character of men.

# Notes on Text

THE TEXTS given here are from the original publications: the essays on poetry in the *Monthly Repository* (1833), the essay on Tennyson in the *London Review* (1835), and the one on de Vigny in the *Westminster Review* (1838). The comment on *Pauline* is from a copy of the poem in the Victoria and Albert Museum.

The essays on poetry and on de Vigny were included in the first volume of the collected essays, *Dissertations and Discussions: Political, Philosophical, and Historical* published in two volumes by John W. Parker in London in 1859. A third volume of essays was added in 1867 and a fourth in 1875, but no changes were made in the first two volumes. A new edition appeared in 1875, two years after Mill's death, under the imprint of Longmans, Green, Reader, and Dyer, but it contains no substantive variants from the 1859 edition, although punctuation and spelling are occasionally altered. Nor are there significant variants in the first American edition: Boston, William V. Spencer, 1864.

Mill's willingness to reprint these essays at a time when his name was much more widely known testifies to the importance Mill attributed to them, and the absence of major revisions suggests a consistency in his views on these matters. What changes do occur are largely stylistic. When a passage is altered in meaning, it is usually in the direction of a more moderate, less dogmatic tone. The largest change is the excision of several paragraphs at the end of the essay "What is Poetry?" Important passages not reprinted in later editions are marked in this text by brackets.

ESSAYS ON POETRY BY *John Stuart Mill*

# 1
# What is Poetry?

The mental crisis altered radically Mill's relation to the utilitarian movement, especially to the utilitarianism of his father, Bentham, and the contributors to the WESTMINSTER during its early years. After 1828 Mill disengaged himself from these associates and in the next years came under a variety of new influences: Goethe, Comte, the Saint Simonians, Carlyle, Coleridge (though as far as one can tell, not his literary criticism), Maurice, and Sterling.

Most significant for the development of both Mill's interest in poetry and the critical essays of 1833 was Mill's entrance into the circle of writers associated with the MONTHLY REPOSITORY. This journal was acquired in 1831 by William Johnson Fox, a Unitarian clergyman and liberal political essayist and literary critic. Fox had been a contributor to the WESTMINSTER during its early years and was acquainted with both James Mill and Bentham. John Mill and Fox probably met in 1824, but Fox's greatest influence upon Mill comes between 1830 and 1833. At Fox's house Mill encountered a number of people with a serious interest in literature: Eliza and Sarah Flower, poetesses and contributors to the REPOSITORY; Harriet Martineau; and his future wife, Harriet Taylor. It is to her that Mill gave the credit for his interest in poetry.

The first years of my friendship with her were, in respect of my own development, mainly years of poetic culture. It is

3

hardly necessary to say that I am not now speaking of *written* poetry, either metrical or otherwise; though I did cultivate this taste as well as a taste for paintings & sculptures, & did read with enthusiasm her favorite poets, especially the one whom she placed far above all others, Shelley. But this was merely accessary. The real poetic culture was, that my faculties, such as they were, became more & more attuned to the beautiful & elevated, in all kinds, & especially in human feeling & character & more capable of vibrating in unison with it.[1]

*Such statements must be read with a due awareness of Mill's habitual overstatement of his indebtedness to Mrs. Taylor. It was at Fox's request that Mill read Browning's* PAULINE, *and it seems likely that Fox both encouraged the two essays on poetry and called Mill's attention to the relatively unknown Tennyson.*

*This essay appeared originally in the* MONTHLY REPOSITORY *for January 1833 (n.s. VII: 60–70). It and the essay "The Two Kinds of Poetry" were published together in volume I of* DISSERTATIONS AND DISCUSSIONS *under the title "Thoughts on Poetry and Its Varieties."*

---

IT HAS OFTEN BEEN ASKED, What is Poetry? And many and various are the answers which have been returned. The vulgarest of all—one with which no person possessed of the faculties to which Poetry addresses itself can ever have been satisfied—is that which confounds poetry with metrical composition: yet to this wretched mockery of a definition, many have been led back, by the failure of all their attempts to find any other that would distinguish what they have been accustomed to call poetry, from much which they have known only under other names.

That, however, the word "poetry" *does* import something quite peculiar in its nature, something which may exist in what

[1] John Stuart Mill, *The Early Draft of John Stuart Mill's Autobiography*, ed. Jack Stillinger (Urbana, 1961), p. 199.

4

is called prose as well as in verse, something which does not even require the instrument of words, but can speak through those other audible symbols called musical sounds, and even through the visible ones, which are the language of sculpture, painting, and architecture; all this, as we believe, is and must be felt, though perhaps indistinctly, by all upon whom poetry in any of its shapes produces any impression beyond that of tickling the ear. To the mind, poetry is either nothing, or it is the better part of all art whatever, and of real life too; and the distinction between poetry and what is not poetry, whether explained or not, is felt to be fundamental.

Where every one feels a difference, a difference there must be. All other appearances may be fallacious, but the appearance of a difference is itself a real difference. Appearances too, like other things, must have a cause, and that which can *cause* anything, even an illusion, must be a reality. And hence, while a half-philosophy disdains the classifications and distinctions indicated by popular language, philosophy carried to its highest point may frame new ones, but never sets aside the old, content with correcting and regularizing them. It cuts fresh channels for thought, but it does not fill up such as it finds ready made, but traces, on the contrary, more deeply, broadly, and distinctly, those into which the current has spontaneously flowed.

Let us then attempt, in the way of modest inquiry, not to coerce and confine nature within the bounds of an arbitrary definition, but rather to find the boundaries which she herself has set, and erect a barrier round them; not calling mankind to account for having misapplied the word "poetry," but attempting to clear up to them the conception which they already attach to it, and to bring before their minds as a distinct *principle* that which, as a vague *feeling*, has really guided them in their actual employment of the term.

The object of poetry is confessedly to act upon the emotions; and therein is poetry sufficiently distinguished from what Wordsworth affirms to be its logical opposite, namely, not prose, but matter of fact or science.[2] The one addresses itself to the belief, the other to the feelings. The one does not work by convincing or persuading, the other by moving. The one acts by presenting a proposition to the understanding, the other by offering interesting objects of contemplation to the sensibilities.

This, however, leaves us very far from a definition of poetry. We have distinguished it from one thing, but we are bound to distinguish it from everything. To present thoughts or images to the mind for the purpose of acting upon the emotions, does not belong to poetry alone. It is equally the province (for example) of the novelist: and yet the faculty of the poet and the faculty of the novelist are as distinct as any other two faculties; as the faculty of the novelist and of the orator, or of the poet and the metaphysician. The two characters may be united, as characters the most disparate may; but they have no natural connexion.

Many of the finest poems are in the form of novels, and in almost all good novels there is true poetry. But there is a radical distinction between the interest felt in a novel as such, and the interest excited by poetry; for the one is derived from *incident*, the other from the representation of *feeling*. In one, the source of the emotion excited is the exhibition of a state or states of human sensibility; in the other, of a series of states of mere outward circumstances. Now, all minds are capable of being affected more or less by representations of the latter kind, and all, or almost all, by those of the former; yet the two sources

2 Wordsworth's Preface to the *Lyrical Ballads*. There are a number of similarities between Mill's views and Wordsworth's. Mill is particularly interested in Wordsworth's claim that poetry and science are compatible parts of the same broader truth: "The man of science seeks truth as a remote and unknown benefactor; he cherishes and loves it in his solitude: the poet, singing a song in which all human beings join with him, rejoices in the presence of truth as our visible friends and hourly companion. Poetry is the breath and finer spirit of all knowledge; it is the impassioned expression which is in the countenance of all science."

of interest correspond to two distinct and (as respects their greatest development) mutually exclusive characters of mind. [So much is the nature of poetry dissimilar to the nature of fictitious narrative, that to have a really strong passion for either of the two, seems to presuppose or to superinduce a comparative indifference to the other.] ³

At what age is the passion for a story, for almost any kind of story, merely as a story, the most intense—in childhood. But that also is the age at which poetry, even of the simplest description, is least relished and least understood; because the feelings with which it is especially conversant are yet undeveloped, and not having been even in the slightest degree experienced, cannot be sympathised with. In what stage of the progress of society, again, is story-telling most valued, and the story-teller in greatest request and honour?—in a rude state; like that of the Tartars and Arabs at this day, and of almost all nations in the earliest ages. But in this state of society there is little poetry except ballads, which are mostly narrative, that is, essentially *stories*, and derive their principal interest from the *incidents*. Considered as poetry, they are of the lowest and most elementary kind: the feelings depicted, or rather indicated, are the simplest our nature has; such joys and griefs as the immediate pressure of some outward event excites in rude minds, which live wholly immersed in outward things, and have never, either from choice or a force they could not resist, turned themselves to the contemplation of the world within. Passing now from childhood, and from the childhood of society, to the grown-up men and women of this most grown-up and unchildlike age—the minds and hearts of greatest depth and elevation are commonly those which take greatest delight in poetry; the shallowest and emptiest, on the contrary, are, by universal remark, the most addicted to novel-reading. This accords, too, with all analogous experience of human nature.

³ Brackets indicate significant passages deleted by Mill from the 1859 edition.

The sort of persons whom not merely in books but in their lives, we find perpetually engaged in hunting for excitement from without, are invariably those who do not possess, either in the vigour of their intellectual powers or in the depth of their sensibilities, that which would enable them to find ample excitement nearer at home. The same persons whose time is divided between sight-seeing, gossip, and fashionable dissipation, take a natural delight in fictitious narrative; the excitement it affords is of the kind which comes from without. Such persons are rarely lovers of poetry, though they may fancy themselves so, because they relish novels in verse. But poetry, which is the delineation of the deeper and more secret workings of the human heart, is interesting only to those to whom it recals [sic] what they have felt, or whose imagination it stirs up to conceive what they could feel, or what they might have been able to feel, had their outward circumstances been different.[4]

Poetry, when it is really such, is truth; and fiction also, if it is good for anything, is truth: but they are different truths. The truth of poetry is to paint the human soul truly: the truth of fiction is to give a true picture of *life*. The two kinds of knowledge are different, and come by different ways, come mostly to different persons. Great poets are often proverbially ignorant of life. What they know has come by observation of themselves; they have found *there* one highly delicate, and sensitive, and refined specimen of human nature, on which the laws of human emotion are written in large characters, such as can be read off without much study: and other knowledge of mankind, such as comes to men of the world by outward experience, is not indispensable to them as poets: but to the novelist such knowledge is

---

[4] The romantic aspects of Mill's poetic theory have been widely recognized since they were pointed out by M. H. Abrams in his well-known study of romantic poetics, *The Mirror and the Lamp*. Mill's theory is a paradigm of Abrams' "expressive" mode. Here, for example, the creative impetus of the poet is from inside his own being, and the poetry itself is an expression of these feelings.

8

all in all; he has to describe outward things, not the inward man; actions and events, not feelings; and it will not do for him to be numbered among those who, as Madame Roland said of Brissot, know man but not *men*.[5]

All this is no bar to the possibility of combining both elements, poetry and narrative or incident, in the same work, and calling it either a novel or a poem; but so may red and white combine on the same human features, or on the same canvass; and so may oil and vinegar, though opposite natures, blend together in the same composite taste. There is one order of composition which requires the union of poetry and incident, each in its highest kind—the dramatic. Even there the two elements are perfectly distinguishable, and may exist of unequal quality, and in the most various proportion. The incidents of a dramatic poem may be scanty and ineffective, though the delineation of passion and character may be of the highest order; as in Goethe's glorious "Torquato Tasso";[6] or again, the story as a mere story may be well got up for effect, as is the case with some of the most trashy productions of the Minerva press; it may even be, what those are not, a coherent and probable series of events, though there be scarcely a feeling exhibited which is not exhibited falsely, or in a manner absolutely common-place. The combination of the two excellencies is what renders Shakspeare so generally acceptable, each sort of readers finding in him what is suitable to their faculties. To the many he is great as a story-teller, to the few as a poet.

In limiting poetry to the delineation of states of feeling, and denying the name where nothing is delineated but outward objects, we may be thought to have done what we promised to

---

[5] Madame Roland in her *Memoires* published in 1820. Jacques Pierre Brissot was an active member of the Girondist party. Mill had a detailed knowledge of the French Revolution and had at one time considered writing a formal history of this period.

[6] Goethe's drama deals with a theme which always interested Mill: the conflict between the gifts of poetic sensibility and the unappreciative world. See Mill's comments below on the similar situation of Alfred de Vigny, ch. 5.

avoid—to have not *found*, but *made* a definition, in opposition
to the usage of the English language, since it is established by
common consent that there is a poetry called *descriptive*. We
deny the charge. Description is not poetry because there is de-
scriptive poetry, no more than science is poetry because there
is such a thing as a didactic poem; no more, we might almost
say, than Greek or Latin is poetry because there are Greek and
Latin poems. But an object which admits of being described, or
a truth which may fill a place in a scientific treatise, may *also*
furnish an occasion for the generation of poetry, which we
thereupon choose to call descriptive or didactic. The poetry is
not in the object itself, nor in the scientific truth itself, but in
the state of mind in which the one and the other may be con-
templated. The mere delineation of the dimensions and colours
of external objects is not poetry, no more than a geometrical
ground-plan of St. Peter's or Westminster Abbey is painting.
Descriptive poetry consists, no doubt, in description, but in de-
scription of things as they appear, not as they *are*; and it paints
them not in their bare and natural lineaments, but arranged in
the colours and seen through the medium of the imagination
set in action by the feelings. If a poet is to describe a lion, he
will not set about describing him as a naturalist would, nor even
as a traveller would, who was intent upon stating the truth, the
whole truth, and nothing but the truth. He will describe him by
*imagery*, that is, by suggesting the most striking likenesses and
contrasts which might occur to a mind contemplating the lion,
in the state of awe, wonder, or terror, which the spectacle
naturally excites, or is, on the occasion, supposed to excite.
Now this is describing the lion professedly, but the state of ex-
citement of the spectator really. The lion may be described
falsely or in exaggerated colours, and the poetry be all the bet-
ter; but if the human emotion be not painted with the most
scrupulous truth, the poetry is bad poetry, i.e. is not poetry at
all, but a failure.

*10*

Thus far our progress towards a clear view of the essentials of poetry has brought us very close to the last two attempts at a definition of poetry which we happen to have seen in print, both of them by poets and men of genius. The one is by Ebenezer Elliott, the author of "Corn-Law Rhymes," and other poems of still greater merit. "Poetry," says he, "is impassioned truth." The other is by a writer in Blackwood's Magazine, and comes, we think still nearer the mark. We forget his exact words, but in substance he defined poetry "man's thoughts tinged by his feelings." There is in either definition a near approximation to what we are in search of. Every truth which man can announce, every thought, even every outward impression, which can enter into his consciousness, may become poetry when shewn through any impassioned medium, when invested with the colouring of joy, or grief, or pity, or affection, or admiration, or reverence, or awe, or even hatred or terror: and, unless so coloured, nothing, be it as interesting as it may, is poetry. But both these definitions fail to discriminate between poetry and eloquence. Eloquence, as well as poetry, is impassioned truth; eloquence, as well as poetry, is thoughts coloured by the feelings. Yet common apprehension and philosophic criticism alike recognize a distinction between the two: there is much that every one would call eloquence, which no one would think of classing as poetry. A question will sometimes arise, whether some particular author is a poet; and those who maintain the negative commonly allow, that though not a poet, he is a highly *eloquent* writer.

The distinction between poetry and eloquence appears to us to be equally fundamental with the distinction between poetry and narrative, or between poetry and description. It is still farther from having been satisfactorily cleared up than either of the others, [unless, which is highly probably, the German artists and critics have thrown some light upon it which has not yet reached us. Without a perfect knowledge of what they have written, it is something like presumption to write upon such subjects at all, and we shall be the foremost to urge that, whatever we may be about to submit, may be received, subject to correction from *them*].

Poetry and eloquence are both alike the expression or uttering forth of feeling. But if we may be excused the seeming affectation of the antithesis, we should say that eloquence is *heard*, poetry is *over*heard. Eloquence supposes an audience; the peculiarity of poetry appears to us to lie in the poet's utter unconsciousness of a listener. Poetry is feeling confessing itself to itself, in moments of solitude, and bodying itself forth in symbols which are the nearest possible representations of the feeling in the exact shape in which it exists in the poet's mind.[7] Eloquence is feeling pouring itself forth to other minds, courting their sympathy, or endeavoring to influence their belief, or move them to passion or to action.

All poetry is of the nature of soliloquy. It may be said that poetry, which is printed on hot-pressed paper, and sold at a book-seller's shop, is a soliloquy in full dress, and upon the stage. But there is nothing absurd in the idea of such a mode of soliloquizing. What we have said to ourselves, we may tell to others afterwards; what we have said or done in solitude, we may voluntarily reproduce when we know that other eyes are upon us. But no trace of consciousness that any eyes are upon us must be visible in the work itself. The actor knows that there is an audience present; but if he act as though he knew it, he acts ill. A poet may write poetry with the intention of publishing it; he may write it even for the express purpose of being

---

[7] This view, as Abrams had pointed out, is similar to that often characterized by Eliot's phrase "objective correlative": "The only way of expressing emotion in the form of art is by finding an 'objective correlative'; in other words, a set of objects, a situation, a chain of events which shall be the formula of that particular emotion; such that when the external facts, which must terminate in sensory experience, are given, the emotion is immediately evoked." (T. S. Eliot, "Hamlet" in *Selected Essays* [London, 1951], p. 145.)

paid for it; that it should *be* poetry, being written under any such influences, is far less probable; not, however, impossible; but no otherwise [sic] possible than if he can succeed in secluding from his work every vestige of such lookings-forth into the outward and every-day world and can express his feelings exactly as he has felt them in solitude, or as he feels that he should feel them, though they were to remain for ever unuttered. But when he turns round and addresses himself to another person; when the act of utterance is not itself the end, but a means to an end,—viz., by the feelings he himself expresses to work upon the feelings, or upon the belief, or the will of another,—when the expression of his emotions, or of his thoughts, tinged by his emotions, is tinged also by that purpose, by that desire of making an impression upon another mind, then it ceases to be poetry, and becomes eloquence.[8]

Poetry, accordingly, is the natural fruit of solitude and meditation; eloquence, of intercourse with the world. The persons who have most feeling of their own, if intellectual culture have given them a language in which to express it, have the highest faculty of poetry; those who best understand the feelings of others, are the most eloquent. The persons, and the nations, who commonly excel in poetry, are those whose character and tastes render them least dependent for their happiness upon the applause, or sympathy, or concurrence of the world in general. Those to whom that applause, that sympathy, that concurrence are most necessary, generally excel most in eloquence. And hence, perhaps, the French, who are the *least* poetical of all great and refined nations, are among the *most* eloquent: the French, also, being the most sociable, the vainest, and the least self-dependent.[9]

[8] Eloquence is what Abrams calls "pragmatic"; poetry is pure of self-consciousness.

[9] It is French neoclassicism to which Mill apparently objects; poetry in which form dominates feeling, which is imitative, conventional, ornamental, and therefore, in Mill's view, insincere.

If the above be, as we believe, the true theory of the distinction commonly admitted between eloquence and poetry; or though it be not that, yet if, as we cannot doubt, the distinction above stated be a real *bona fide* distinction, it will be found to hold, not merely in the language of words, but in all other language, and to intersect the whole domain of art.

Take, for example, music: we shall find in that art, so peculiarly the expression of passion, two perfectly distinct styles; one of which may be called the poetry, the other the oratory of music. This difference being seized would put an end to much musical sectarianism. There has been much contention whether the character of Rossini's music—the music, we mean, which is characteristic of that composer—is compatible with the expression of passion. Without doubt, the passion it expresses is not the musing, meditative tenderness, or pathos, or grief of Mozart, the great poet of his art. Yet it is passion, but *garrulous* passion—the passion which pours itself into other ears; and therein the better calculated for *dramatic* effect, having a natural adaptation for dialogue. Mozart also is great in musical oratory; but his most touching compositions are in the opposite style—that of soliloquy. Who can imagine "Dove sono" *heard?*[10] We imagine it *over*-heard. [The same is the case with many of the finest national airs. Who can hear those words, which speak so touchingly the sorrows of a mountaineer in exile:—

> "My heart's in the Highlands—my heart is not here:
> My heart's in the Highlands, a-chasing the deer.
> A-chasing the wild-deer, and following the roe—
> My heart's in the Highlands, wherever I go."

Who can hear those affecting words, married to as affecting an air, and fancy that he *sees* the singer? That song has always seemed to us like the lament of a prisoner in a solitary cell, ourselves listening, unseen in the next. As the direct opposite of

[10] Act III of *The Marriage of Figaro*.

this, take "Scots wha hae wi' Wallace bled," where the music is as oratorical as the poetry.]

Purely pathetic music commonly partakes of soliloquy. The soul is absorbed in its distress, and though there may be by-standers, it is not thinking of them. When the mind is looking within, and not without, its state does not often or rapidly vary; and hence the even, uninterrupted flow, approaching almost to monotony, which a good reader, or a good singer, will give to words or music of a pensive or melancholy cast. But grief, taking the form of a prayer, or of a complaint, becomes oratorical; no longer low, and even, and subdued, it assumes a more emphatic rhythm, a more rapidly returning accent; instead of a few slow, equal notes, following one after another at regular intervals, it crowds note upon note, and ofttimes assumes a hurry and bustle like joy. Those who are familiar with some of the best of Rossini's serious compositions, such as the air "Tu che i miseri conforti," in the opera of "Tancredi," or the duet "Ebben per mia memoria," in "La Gazza Ladra," will at once understand and feel our meaning.[11] Both are highly tragic and passionate; the passion of both is that of oratory, not poetry. The like may be said of that most moving prayer in Beethoven's "Fidelio"—

> "Komm, Hoffnung, lass das letzte Stern
> Der Müde nicht erbleichen;"[12]

in which Madame Devrient,[13] last summer, exhibited such consummate powers of pathetic expression. How different from

---

[11] *Tancredi* is Rossini's first work (1813). At the opening of Act II, Isaura, confidante of the imprisoned Amenaide, consoles her by suggesting she have faith in Tancredi's love. The duet from *La Gazza Ladra* is between Ninetta and Pippo at the opening of Act II. Ninetta is also falsely accused and imprisoned as was Amenaide.

[12] Leonora's aria: "Come, Hope, do not let the last sorrowful but consoling star of love grow dim." It is curious that all three of these examples involve the attempted consolation of good people imprisoned for holding to their beliefs in difficult circumstances.

[13] Madame Wilhelmine Schröder-Devrient (1804–60), one of the best-known operatic singers of the age. Leonora, the role for which she was best known, was sung in London in 1832.

Winter's[14] beautiful "Paga pii," the very soul of melancholy exhaling itself in solitude; fuller of meaning, and, therefore, more profoundly poetical than the words for which it was composed—for it seems to express not simple melancholy, but the melancholy of remorse.

If, from vocal music, we now pass to instrumental, we may have a specimen of musical oratory in any fine military symphony or march: while the poetry of music seems to have attained its consummation in Beethoven's Overture to Egmont. We question whether so deep an expression of mixed grandeur and melancholy was ever in any other instance produced by mere sounds.

In the arts which speak to the eye, the same distinctions will be found to hold, not only between poetry and oratory, but between poetry, oratory, narrative, and simple imitation or description.

Pure *description* is exemplified in a *mere* portrait or a *mere* landscape—productions of art, it is true, but of the mechanical rather than of the fine arts, being works of simple imitation, not *creation*. We say, a *mere* portrait, or a *mere* landscape, because it is possible for a portrait or a landscape, without ceasing to be such, to be also a *picture*. [A portrait by Lawrence,[15] or one of Turner's views, is not a mere copy from nature: the one combines with the given features that particular expression (among all good and pleasing ones) which those features are most capable of wearing, and which, therefore, in combination with them, is capable of producing the greatest positive beauty. Turner, again, unites the objects of the given landscape with whatever sky, and whatever light and shade, enable those particular objects to impress the imagination most strongly. In

[14] Peter Winter (1754–1825), court conductor in Munich and composer of many operatic works.
[15] Sir Thomas Lawrence (1769–1830), principal portrait painter to royalty after the death of Reynolds.

both, there is *creative* art—not working after an actual model, but realizing an idea.]

Whatever in painting or sculpture expresses human feeling, or *character*, which is only a certain state of feeling grown habitual, may be called, according to circumstances, the poetry or the eloquence of the painter's or the sculptor's art; the poetry, if the feeling declares itself by such signs as escape from us when we are unconscious of being seen; the oratory, if the signs are those we use for the purpose of voluntary communication.

[The poetry of painting seems to be carried to its highest perfection in the Peasant Girl of Rembrandt, or in any Madonna or Magdalen of Guido; that of sculpture, in almost any of the Greek statues of the gods; not considering these in respect to the mere physical beauty, of which they are such perfect models, nor undertaking either to vindicate or to contest the opinion of philosophers, that even physical beauty is ultimately resolvable into expression; we may safely affirm, that in no other of man's works did so much of soul ever shine through mere inanimate matter.]

The narrative style answers to what is called historical painting, which it is the fashion among connoisseurs to treat as the climax of the pictorial art. That it is the most difficult branch of the art, we do not doubt, because, in its perfection, it includes, in a manner, the perfection of all the other branches. As an epic poem, though, in so far as it is epic (*i.e.* narrative), it is not poetry at all, is yet esteemed the greatest effort of poetic genius, because there is no kind whatever of poetry which may not appropriately find a place in it. But an historical picture, as such, that is, as the representation of an incident, must necessarily, as it seems to us, be poor and ineffective. The narrative powers of painting are extremely limited. Scarcely any picture, scarcely any series even of pictures, which we know of, tells its own story without the aid of an interpreter; you must know the story beforehand; *then*, indeed you may see great beauty and appropriateness in the painting. But it is the single figures which, to us, are the great charm even of a historical picture.[16] It is in these that the power of the art is really seen: in the attempt to *narrate*, visible and permanent signs are far behind the fugitive audible ones which follow so fast one after another, while the faces and figures in a narrative picture, even though they be Titian's, stand still. Who would not prefer one Virgin and Child of Raphael, to all the pictures which Rubens, with his fat, frouzy Dutch Venuses, ever painted? Though Rubens, besides excelling almost every one in his mastery over all the mechanical parts of his art, often shows real genius in *grouping* his figures, the peculiar problem of historical painting. But, then, who, except a mere student of drawing and colouring, ever cared to look twice at any of the figures themselves? The power of painting lies in poetry, of which Rubens had not the slightest tincture—not in narrative, where he might have excelled.

The single figures, however, in an historical picture, are rather the *eloquence* of painting than the poetry: they mostly (unless they are quite out of place in the picture) express the feelings of one person as modified by the presence of others. Accordingly the minds whose bent leads them rather to eloquence than to poetry, rush to historical painting. The French painters, for instance, seldom attempt, because they could make nothing of, single heads, like those glorious ones of the Italian masters, with which they might glut themselves day after day in their own Louvre. They must all be *historical*; and

[16] Mill's review of Carlyle's *The French Revolution* (1837) discusses the various kinds of historical writing, praising Carlyle for writing the "authentic History and the Poetry of the French Revolution" at the same time. Carlyle has been able to go beyond the "dry mechanical facts which compose the story" to the "feelings—the high and solemn, the tender or mournful, even the gay and mirthful contemplations, which the story, or the manner of reciting it, awakens in our mind" (*Westminster Review* XXVII [1837]: 21).

they are, almost to a man, attitudinizers. If we wished to give to any young artist the most impressive warning our imaginations could devise, against that kind of vice in the pictorial, which corresponds to rant in the histrionic art, we would advise him to walk once up and down the gallery of the Luxembourg; [even now when David,[17] the great corrupter of taste, has been translated from this world to the next, and from the Luxembourg, consequently, into the more elevated sphere of the Louvre]. Every figure in French painting or statuary seems to be showing itself off before spectators: they are in the worst style of corrupted eloquence, [but in no style of poetry at all. The best are stiff and unnatural; the worst resemble figures of cataleptic patients. The French artists fancy themselves imitators of the classics, yet they seem to have no understanding and no feeling of that *repose* which was the peculiar and pervading character of Grecian art, until it began to decline: a repose tenfold more indicative of strength than all their stretching and straining; for strength, as Thomas Carlyle says, does not manifest itself in spasms.[18]

There are some productions of art which it seems at first difficult to arrange in any of the classes above illustrated. The direct aim of art as such, is the production of the *beautiful*; and as there are other things beautiful besides states of mind, there is much of art which may seem to have nothing to do with either poetry or eloquence as we have defined them. Take for

[17] David's historical paintings (*The Death of Socrates*, *The Oath of the Horatii*, *Leonidas at Thermopylae*) are perhaps the best examples of what Mill is complaining of, and perhaps the imitative work of Gros and Girodet.

[18] Mill's interest in Hellenism as a source of strength is probably taken from Carlyle, who follows the late eighteenth century revival of interest in Greek culture in the work of Winckelmann and Goethe. Mill later (1854) specifically disavows the idea: "Not symmetry, but bold, free expansion in all directions is demanded by the needs of modern life and the instincts of the modern mind. Great and strong and varied faculties are more wanted than faculties well proportioned to one another; a Hercules or a Briareus more than an Apollo" (Mill, *The Letters of John Stuart Mill*, ed. Elliot, II: 268).

*19*

instance a composition of Claude, or Salvator Rosa.[19] There is here *creation* of new beauty: by the grouping of natural scenery, conformably indeed to the laws of outward nature, but not after any actual model; the result being a beauty more perfect and faultless than is perhaps to be found in any actual landscape. Yet there is a character of poetry even in these, without which they could not be so beautiful. The unity, and wholeness, and æsthetic congruity of the picture still lies in singleness of expression; but it is expression in a different sense from that in which we have hitherto employed the term. The objects in an imaginary landscape cannot be said, like the words of a poem or the notes of a melody, to be the actual utterance of a feeling; but there must be some feeling with which they harmonize, and which they have a tendency to raise up in the spectator's mind. They must inspire a feeling of grandeur, a loveliness, a cheerfulness, a wildness, a melancholy, a terror. The painter must surround his principal objects with such imagery as would spontaneously arise in a highly imaginative mind, when contemplating those objects under the impression of the feelings which they are intended to inspire. This, if it be not poetry, is so nearly allied to it, as scarcely to require being distinguished.

In this sense we may speak of the poetry of architecture. All architecture, to be impressive, must be the expression or symbol of some interesting idea; some thought, which has power over the emotions. The reason why modern architecture is so paltry, is simply that it is not the expression of any idea; it is a mere parroting of the architectural tongue of the Greeks, or of our Teutonic ancestors, without any conception of a meaning.

To confine ourselves, for the present, to religious edifices:

---

[19] Mill's interest in the particular physical stimuli that give rise to these emotions, to what is sometimes called the "picturesque," is carried on in his notes to the edition of his father's *Analysis of the Phenomena of the Human Mind* published in 1869 Here he denies any inherent physical source for aesthetic emotion, attributing it to certain "Ideas" which, when present in poetry, supply the particular emotion. This discussion includes interesting references to the aesthetics of Coleridge and Ruskin.

*20*

these partake of poetry, in proportion as they express, or har-
monize with, the feelings of devotion. But those feelings are
different according to the conception entertained of the beings,
by whose supposed nature they are called forth. To the Greek,
these beings were incarnations of the greatest conceivable
physical beauty, combined with supernatural power: and the
Greek temples express this, their predominant character being
graceful strength; in other words, solidity, which is power, and
lightness which is also power, accomplishing with small means
what seemed to require great; to combine all in one word,
*majesty*. To the Catholic, again, the Deity was something far
less clear and definite; a being of still more resistless power than
the heathen divinities; greatly to be loved; still more greatly to
be feared; and wrapped up in vagueness, mystery, and incom-
prehensibility. A certain solemnity, a feeling of doubting and
trembling hope, like that of one lost in a boundless forest who
thinks he knows his way but is not sure, mixes itself in all the
genuine expressions of Catholic devotion. This is eminently the
expression of the pure Gothic cathedral; conspicuous equally in
the mingled majesty and gloom of its vaulted roofs and stately
aisles, and in the "dim religious light" which steals through its
painted windows.[20]

There is no generic distinction between the imagery which
is the *expression* of feeling and the imagery which is felt to
*harmonize* with feeling. They are identical. The imagery in
which feeling utters itself forth from within, is also that in
which it delights when presented to it from without. All art,
therefore, in proportion as it produces its effects by an appeal

---

[20] Mill's response to Gothic architecture reflects the "dim religious light" of his
own time and its "doubting and trembling hope." Modern studies suggest that the
cathedral expressed the certainty of the faith of its builders, that there was nothing
doubtful about it. "Above all," writes von Simpson, "the cathedral was the intimation of
ineffable truth." Moreover, light, far from being an aesthetic matter, "conveyed an in-
sight into the perfection of the cosmos, and a divination of the Creator." (Otto von
Simpson, *The Gothic Cathedral* [New York, 1956], pp. 35, 51).

to the emotions partakes of poetry, unless it partakes of oratory, or of narrative. And the distinction which these three words indicate, runs through the whole field of the fine arts.

The above hints have no pretension to the character of a theory. They are merely thrown out for the consideration of thinkers, in the hope that if they do not contain the truth, they may do somewhat to suggest it. Nor would they, crude as they are, have been deemed worthy of publication, in any country but one in which the philosophy of art is so completely neglected, that whatever may serve to put any inquiring mind upon this kind of investigation, cannot well, however imperfect in itself, fail altogether to be of use.

ANTIQUUS.]

# 2
# Browning's
# *Pauline*

PAULINE *was the first published work of Robert Browning, appearing in March 1833, when the poet was twenty. In an effort to gain some critical notice and thus launch his literary career, Browning appealed to William Johnson Fox. There were several connections between them: ten years before, the Browning family had attended the Unitarian chapel where Fox was preaching; and Eliza and Sarah Flower, whose guardian Fox now was, had also been youthful acquaintances of Browning. In fact, in 1824 Eliza had shown Browning's juvenile manuscript ("Incondita") to Fox, who had made encouraging remarks about it. Now, in 1833, Fox was editor of the* MONTHLY REPOSITORY *and in a position to give the aspiring poet some practical assistance.*

*Accordingly Fox gave the poem a lengthy and favorable review in the April issue, but his efforts to distribute for notice elsewhere the dozen copies Browning had sent were less successful. One of these copies went to Mill, with the hope that he could place notices in Fonblanque's* EXAMINER *and* TAIT'S EDINBURGH MAGAZINE, *both of which had published Mill's work.*

*Mill and Mrs. Taylor read the poem together, both inserting brief marginal comments, and Mill made some further observations in the flyleaves. Mill also appears to have composed a short review for publication. He refers, in a letter to Carlyle in July 1833, to his continuing study of poetry: "I think I men-*

Flyleaves of Mill's copy of Browning's *Pauline*.
By courtesy of the Victoria and Albert Museum.

— write had made, as yet, only the next
step; viz. into despising his own state. I even
question whether part even of that self-disdain
is not assumed. He is evidently dissatisfied,
and feels part of the badness of his state, but
He does not write as if it were purged out
of him — if he once could muster a hearty
hatred of this selfishness, it would go — and
he feels only the lack of good, not the pointed
evil. He feels not remorse, but only disappointment.
A mind in that state can only be regenerated
by some new passion, and I know not what
to wish for him but that he may meet with
a real Pauline —

Meanwhile he should not attempt to
shew how a person may be recovered from
this morbid state — for he is hardly
convalescent, and 'what should we speak
of but that which we know?'

*tioned to you that I have carried the investigation (rightly or wrongly as it may be) one step further in a paper (being a review of a new poem) which I wrote for the* EXAMINER: *it proved too long for Fonblanque, and it is to appear in Tait. . . ." But for some reason the review never appeared, and the text has been lost.*

*As far as Mill was concerned the matter was closed when in October he returned the review copy to Fox, noting that "on the whole the observations are not flattering to the author—perhaps too strong in the expression to be shown to him."* [1] *But despite Mill's caution, Fox showed Mill's comments to the poet, on whom they made a deep impression. Tradition, indeed, has credited Mill with causing a radical change in Browning's poetic mode, turning the poet to new technical experiments aimed at achieving a more objective and less personal and self-conscious voice.* [2] *Browning did not reprint the poem until 1868 and then only with a preface discounting it as a juvenile experiment. That version does, however, adopt a number of the changes put in the margins in response to Mill's criticisms in 1833.*

*The brief note in pencil appears on flyleaves in the back of the copy of the poem in the Forster and Dyce Collection of the Victoria and Albert Museum. The text given here reproduces Mill's informal punctuation as exactly as possible. A few words are incomplete, but the intention is clear.*

---

WITH CONSIDERABLE POETIC POWERS, this writer seems to me possessed with a more intense and morbid self-consciousness than I ever knew in any sane human being. I should think it a

[1] Mill, *Earlier Letters*, p. 162; F. A. Hayek, *John Stuart Mill and Harriet Taylor* (Chicago, 1951), p. 43. An account of the history of this particular volume and a list of marginalia by Mill and by Mrs. Taylor, and Browning's responses to them is given by William S. Petersen and Frederick Standley, "The J. S. Mill Marginalia in Robert Browning's *Pauline*: a History and Transcription," in *Papers of the Bibliographic Society of America* LXVI (1972): 135–70.

[2] A contrasting version of the importance of Mill's remarks to Browning is given by Masao Myoshi, "Mill and 'Pauline': the Myth and some Facts," *Victorian Studies* IX (1965): 154–63.

*sincere confession* though of a most unloveable [sic] state, if the 'Pauline' were not evidently a mere phantom. All about *her* is full of inconsistency—he neither loves her nor fancies he loves her, yet insists upon *talking* love to her—if she *existed* and loved him, he treats her most ungenerously and unfeelingly. All his aspirings and yearnings and regrets point to other things, never to her—then he *pays her off* towards the end by a piece of flummery, amounting to the modest request that she will love him and live with him and give herself up to him *without* his *loving her, moyennant quoi* he will think her and call her everything that is handsome and he promises her that she shall find it mighty pleasant. Then he leaves off by saying he knows he shall have changed his mind by tomorrow & despises 'these intents which seem so fair' but that having been thus visited once no doubt he will again—& is therefore 'in perfect joy' bad luck to him! as the Irish say.

A cento of most beautiful passages might be made from this poem—& the psychological history of himself is powerful and truthful, *truth-like* certainly all but the last stage. *That* he evidently has not yet got into. The self-seeking & self-worshipping state is well described—beyond that I should think the writer had made, as yet, only the next step, viz. into despising his own state. I even question whether part even of that self-disdain is not *assumed*. He is evidently *dissatisfied*, and feels part of the badness of his state, he does not write as if it were purged out of him—if he once could muster a hearty hatred of his selfishness, it would *go*—as it i[s] he feels only the *lack* of *good*, not the positive evil. He feels not remorse, but only disappointm[ent] a mind in that state can only be regenerate[d] by some new passion, and I know not what to wish for him but that he may meet with a *real* Pauline.

Meanwhile he should not attempt to shew how a person may be *recovered* from this morbid state—for *he* is hardly convalescent, and 'what should we speak of but that which we know?'

# 3
# The Two Kinds
# of Poetry

*After the appearance of "What is Poetry?" in January 1833, Mill had some second thoughts, and during the following months he exchanged a number of letters with Carlyle in which literary questions are discussed. Mill acknowledges that "I have not got quite into the heart of that mystery," and that he sees "a not very far distant boundary to all I am qualified to accomplish in* this *particular line of speculation."[1] Carlyle replies in an encouraging vein, describing "What is Poetry?" as "honest" and "considerate." But recognizing the rationalist basis of Mill's discussion, he declines any extensive comment: "No man is less versed in logical Defining than I of late years; and perhaps one may doubt whether Poetry is a thing that Science can* define."[2] *Mill gives qualified agreement: "What you say of that paper of mine of Poetry and Art is exactly what I think respecting it myself. I do not think it contains anything erroneous, but I feel that it is far from going to the bottom of the subject, or even very deep into it; I think I see somewhat further into it now, and shall perhaps understand it in time."[3]*

*In October, Mill sends Carlyle a copy of the* Repository, *calling his attention to the "little paper I told you I was writing*

[1] Mill, *Earlier Letters*, p. 149.
[2] Thomas Carlyle, *Letters of Thomas Carlyle to John Stuart Mill, John Sterling and Robert Browning*, ed. Alexander Carlyle (New York, 1923), p. 59.
[3] Mill, *Earlier Letters*, p. 162.

28

*in further prosecution of, or rather improvement on, the
thoughts I published before on Poetry and Art." Carlyle, Mill
recognizes, will probably find the essay "too much infected by
mechanical theories of the mind: yet you will probably in this as
in many other cases be glad to see that out of my mechanical
premises I elicit dynamical conclusions. . . ."*[4]

This essay appeared in the MONTHLY REPOSITORY *for October*
1833 n.s. (VII: 714–24).

---

NASCITUR POËTA is a maxim of classical antiquity, which has
passed to these latter days with less questioning than most of
the doctrines of that early age. When it originated, the human
faculties were occupied, fortunately for posterity, less in exa-
mining how the works of genius are created, than in creating
them: and the adage, probably, had no higher source than the
tendency, common among mankind, to consider all power
which is not visibly the effect of practice, all skill which is not
capable of being reduced to mechanical rules, as the result of a
peculiar gift. Yet this aphorism, born in the infancy of psychol-
ogy, will perhaps be found, now when that science is in its
adolescence, to be as true as an epigram ever is, that is, to con-
tain some truth: truth, however, which has been so compressed
and bent out of shape, in order to tie it up into so small a knot
of only two words, that it requires an almost infinite amount
of unrolling and laying straight, before it will resume its just
proportions.

We are now intending to remark upon the grosser misappli-
cations of this ancient maxim, which have engendered so
many races of poetasters. The days are gone by, when every
raw youth whose borrowed phantasies have set themselves to a
borrowed tune, mistaking as Coleridge says, an ardent desire of
poetic reputation for poetic genius, while unable to disguise

[4] Ibid., p. 181.

from himself that he had taken no means whereby he might
*become* a poet, could fancy himself a born one.[5] Those who
would reap without sowing, and gain the victory without
fighting the battle, are ambitious now of another sort of distinc-
tion, and are born novelists, or public speakers, not poets. And
the wiser thinkers begin to understand and acknowledge that
poetic excellence is subject to the same necessary conditions
with any other mental endowment; and that to no one of the
spiritual benefactors of mankind is a higher or a more assiduous
intellectual culture needful than to the poet. It is true, he pos-
sesses this advantage over others who use the "instrument of
words," that of the truths which he utters, a larger proportion
are derived from personal consciousness, and a smaller from
philosophic investigation. But the power itself of discriminating
between what really is consciousness, and what is only a pro-
cess of inference completed in a single instant; and the capacity
of distinguishing whether that of which the mind is conscious,
be an eternal truth, or but a dream—are among the last results
of the most matured and perfected intellect. Not to mention
that the poet, no more than any other person who writes,
confines himself altogether to intuitive truths, nor has any
means of communicating even these, but by words, every one
of which derives all its power of conveying a meaning, from a
whole host of acquired notions, and facts learnt by study and
experience.

Nevertheless, it seems undeniable in point of fact, and con-
sistent with the principles of a sound metaphysics, that there
are poetic *natures*. There is a mental and physical constitution
or temperament, peculiarly fitted for poetry. This temperament

[5] *Biographia Literaria*, ed. J. Shawcross (Oxford, 1907), I: 25. Both the essays on
poetry suggest the *Biographia* as a source. In the first two chapters Coleridge addresses
himself to the same question of sincerity that Mill is discussing here. Coleridge also de-
scribes his own youthful "delving in the unwholesome quicksilver mines of metaphysic
depths," (*Biographia*, I: 10), a condition that would have recommended him to Mill as a
fellow sufferer of a "mental crisis." Mill's account of his own crisis contains a quotation
from Coleridge's "Dejection: An Ode."

*30*

will not of itself make a poet, no more than the soil will the fruit; and as good fruit may be raised by culture from indifferent soils, so may good poetry from naturally unpoetical minds. But the poetry of one, who is a poet by nature, will be clearly and broadly distinguishable from the poetry of mere culture. It may not be truer; it may not be more useful; but it will be different: fewer will appreciate it, even though many should affect to do so; but in those few it will find a keener sympathy, and will yield them a deeper enjoyment.

One may write genuine poetry, and not be a poet; for whosoever writes out truly any one human feeling, writes poetry. All persons, even the most unimaginative, in moments of strong emotion, speak poetry; and hence the drama is poetry, which else were always prose, except when a poet is one of the characters. What *is* poetry, but the thoughts and words in which emotion spontaneously embodies itself? As there are few who are not, at least for *some* moments and in *some* situations, capable of *some* strong feeling, poetry is natural to most persons at some period of their lives. And any one whose feelings are genuine, though but of the average strength—if he be not diverted by uncongenial thoughts or occupations from the indulgence of them, and if he acquires by culture, as all persons may, the faculty of delineating them correctly,—has it in his power to be a poet, so far as a life passed in writing unquestionable poetry may be considered to confer that title. But *ought* it to do so? yes, perhaps, in the table of contents of a collection of "British Poets." But "poet" is the name also of a variety of *man*, not solely of the author of a particular variety of *book*: now, to have written whole volumes of real poetry is possible to almost all kinds of characters, and implies no greater peculiarity of mental construction, than to be the author of a history, or a novel.

Whom, then, shall we call poets? Those who are so constituted, that emotions are the links of association by which their

31

ideas, both sensuous and spiritual, are connected together. This constitution belongs (within certain limits) to all in whom poetry is a prevading principle. In all others, poetry is something extraneous and superinduced: something out of themselves, foreign to the habitual course of their every-day lives and characters; a quite other world, to which they may make occasional visits, but where they are sojourners, not dwellers, and which, when out of it, or even when in it, they think of, peradventure, but as a phantom-world, a place of *ignes fatui* and spectral illusions. Those only who have the peculiarity of association which we have mentioned, and which is one of the natural consequences of intense sensibility, instead of seeming not themselves when they are uttering poetry, scarcely seem themselves when uttering any thing to which poetry is foreign. Whatever be the thing which they are contemplating, the aspect under which it first and most naturally paints itself to them, is its poetic aspect. The poet of culture sees his object in prose, and describes it in poetry; the poet of nature actually sees it in poetry.

This point is perhaps worth some little illustration; the rather, as metaphysicians (the ultimate arbiters of all philosophical criticism) while they have busied themselves for two thousand years, more or less, about the few *universal* laws of human nature, have strangely neglected the analysis of its *diversities*. Of these, none lie deeper or reach further than the varieties which difference of nature and of education makes in what may be termed the habitual bond of association. In a mind entirely uncultivated, which is also without any strong feelings, objects whether of sense or of intellect arrange themselves in the mere casual order in which they have been seen, heard, or otherwise perceived. Persons of this sort may be said to think chronologically. If they remember a fact, it is by reason of a fortuitous coincidence with some trifling incident or circumstance which took place at the very time. If they have a story to tell, or testimony to deliver in a witness-box, their narrative must follow the exact order in which the events took place: *dodge* them, and the thread of association is broken; they cannot go on. Their associations, to use the language of philosophers, are chiefly of the successive, not the synchronous kind, and whether successive or synchronous, are mostly *casual*.

To the man of science, again, or of business, objects group themselves according to the artificial classifications which the understanding has voluntarily made for the convenience of thought or of practice. But where any of the impressions are vivid and intense, the associations into which these enter are the ruling ones: it being a well-known law of association, that the stronger a feeling is, the more rapidly and strongly it associates itself with any other object or feeling. Where, therefore, nature has given strong feelings, and education has not created factitious tendencies stronger than the natural ones, the prevailing associations will be those which connect objects and ideas with emotions, and with each other through the intervention of emotions. Thoughts and images will be linked together, according to the similarity of the feelings which cling to them. A thought will introduce a thought by first introducing a feeling which is allied with it. At the centre of each group of thoughts or images will be found a feeling: and the thoughts or images are only there because the feeling was there. All the combinations which the mind puts together, all the pictures which it paints, all the wholes which Imagination constructs out of the materials supplied by Fancy, will be indebted to some dominant *feeling*, not as in other natures to a dominant *thought*, for their unity and consistency of character, for what distinguishes them from incoherencies.

The difference, then, between the poetry of a poet, and the poetry of a cultivated but not naturally poetical mind is that in the latter, with however bright a halo of feeling the thought may be surrounded and glorified, the thought itself is still the conspicuous object; while the poetry of a poet is Feeling itself, employing Thought only as the medium of its utterance. In the one feeling waits upon thought; in the other, thought upon feeling. The one writer has a distinct aim, common to him with any other didactic author; he desires to convey the thought, and he conveys it clothed in the feelings which it excites in himself, or which he deems most appropriate to it. The other merely pours forth the overflowing of his feelings; and all the thoughts which those feelings suggest are floated promiscuously along the stream.

It may assist in rendering our meaning intelligible, if we illustrate it by a parallel between the two English authors of our own day, who have produced the greatest quantity of true and enduring poetry, Wordsworth and Shelley. Apter instances could not be wished for; the one might be cited as the type, the *exemplar*, of what the poetry of culture may accomplish, the other as perhaps the most striking example ever known of the poetic temperament. How different, accordingly, is the poetry of these two great writers! In Wordsworth, the poetry is almost always the mere setting of a thought. The thought may be more valuable than the setting, or it may be less valuable, but there can be no question as to which was first in his mind: what he is impressed with, and what he is anxious to impress, is some proposition, more or less distinctly conceived; some truth, or something which he deems such. He lets the thought dwell in his mind, till it excites, as is the nature of thought, other thoughts, and also such feelings as the measure of his sensibility is adequate to supply. Among these thoughts and feelings, had he chosen a different walk of authorship, (and there are many in which he might equally have excelled,) he would probably have made a different selection of media for enforcing the parent-thought: his habits, however, being those of poetic composition, he selects in preference the strongest

34

feelings and the thoughts with which most of feeling is natur-
ally or habitually connected. His poetry therefore may be
defined to be, his thoughts, coloured by, and impressing them-
selves by means of, emotions. Such poetry, Wordsworth has
occupied a long life in producing. And well and wisely has he
so done. Criticisms, no doubt, may be made occasionally both
upon the thoughts themselves, and upon the skill he has dem-
onstrated in the choice of his *media:* for, an affair of skill and
study, in the most rigorous sense, it evidently was. But he has
not laboured in vain: he has exercised, and continues to exer-
cise, a powerful, and mostly a highly beneficial influence over
the formation and growth of not a few of the most cultivated
and vigorous of the youthful minds of our time, over whose
heads poetry of the opposite description would have flown, for
want of an original organization, physical and mental, in sym-
pathy with it.

On the other hand, Wordsworth's poetry is never bounding,
never ebullient; has little even of the appearance of spontane-
ousness: the well is never so full that it overflows. There is an
air of calm deliberateness about all he writes, which is not
characteristic of the poetic temperament; his poetry seems one
thing, himself another; he seems to be poetical because he wills
to be so, not because he cannot help it: did he will to dismiss
poetry, he need never again, it might almost seem, have a poeti-
cal thought. He never seems *possessed* by a feeling; no emotion
seems ever so strong as to have entire sway, for the time being,
over the current of his thoughts. He never, even for the space
of a few stanzas, appears entirely *given up* to exultation, or
grief, or pity, or love, or admiration, or devotion, or even ani-
mal spirits. He now and then, though seldom, *attempts* to write
as if he were; and never, we think, without leaving an impres-
sion of poverty: as the brook which on nearly level ground quite
fills its banks, appears but a thread when running rapidly down
a precipitous declivity. He has feeling enough to form a decent,

*35*

graceful, even beautiful, decoration, to a thought which is in itself interesting and moving; but not so much as suffices to stir up the soul by mere sympathy with itself in its simplest manifestation, nor enough to summon up that array of "thoughts of power," which in a richly stored mind always attends the call of really intense feeling. It is for this reason, doubtless, that the genius of Wordsworth is essentially unlyrical. Lyric poetry, as it was the earliest kind, is also, if the view we are now taking of poetry be correct, more eminently and peculiarly poetry than any other: it is the poetry most natural to a really poetic temperament, and least capable of being successfully imitated by one not so endowed by nature. [All Wordsworth's attempts in that strain, if we may venture to say so much of a man whom we so exceedingly admire, appear to us cold and spiritless.]

Shelley is the very reverse of all this. Where Wordsworth is strong, he is weak; where Wordsworth is weak, he is strong. Culture, that culture by which Wordsworth has reared from his own inward nature the richest harvest ever brought forth by a soil of so little depth, is precisely what was wanting to Shelley: or let us rather say, he had not, at the period of his deplorably early death, reached sufficiently far in that intellectual progression of which he was capable, and which, if it has done so much for far inferior natures, might have made of him the greatest of our poets. For him, intentional mental discipline had done little; the vividness of his emotions and of his sensations had done all. He seldom follows up an idea; it starts into life, summons from the fairy-land of his inexhaustible fancy some three or four bold images, then vanishes, and straight he is off on the wings of some casual association into quite another sphere. He had not yet acquired the consecutiveness of thought necessary for a long poem; his more ambitious compositions too often resemble the scattered fragments of a mirror; colours brilliant as life, single images without end, but no picture. It is only when under the overruling influence of some one state of

36

feeling, either actually experienced, or summoned up in almost the vividness of reality by a fervid imagination, that he writes as a great poet; unity of feeling being to him the harmonizing principle which a central idea is to minds of another class, and supplying the coherency and consistency which would else have been wanting. Thus it is in many of his smaller, and especially his lyrical poems. They are obviously written to exhale, perhaps to relieve, a state of feeling, or of conception of feeling, almost oppressive from its vividness. The thoughts and imagery are suggested by the feeling, and are such as it finds unsought. The state of feeling may be either of soul or of sense, or oftener (might we not say invariably?) of both; for the poetic temperament is usually, perhaps always, accompanied by exquisite senses. The exciting cause may be either an object or an idea. But whatever of sensation enters into the feeling, must not be local, or consciously bodily; it is a state of the whole frame, not of a part only; like the state of sensation produced by a fine climate, or indeed like all strongly pleasurable or painful sensations in an impassioned nature, it pervades the entire nervous system. States of feeling, whether sensuous or spiritual, which thus possess the whole being, are the fountains of that poetry which we have called the poetry of poets; and which is little else than the utterance of the thoughts and images that pass across the mind while some permanent state of feeling is occupying it.

To the same original fineness of organization, Shelley was doubtless indebted for another of his rarest gifts, that exuberance of imagery, which when unrepressed, as in many of his poems it is, amounts even to a vice. The susceptibility of his nervous system, which made his emotions intense, made also the impressions of his external senses deep and clear: and agreeably to the law of association by which, as already remarked, the strongest impressions are those which associate themselves the most easily and strongly, these vivid sensations were readily recalled to mind by all objects or thoughts which had coexisted with them, by all feelings which in any degree resembled them. Never did a fancy so teem with sensuous imagery as Shelley's. Wordsworth economizes an image, and detains it until he had distilled all the poetry out of it, and it will not yield a drop more: Shelley lavishes his with a profusion which is unconscious because it is inexhaustible. [The one, like a thrifty housewife, uses all his materials and wastes none: the other scatters them with a reckless prodigality of wealth of which there is perhaps no similar instance.]

If, then, the maxim *nascitur poëta*, mean, either that the power of producing poetical compositions is a peculiar faculty which the poet brings into the world with him, which grows with his growth like any of his bodily powers, and is as independent of culture as his height, and his complexion; or that *any* natural peculiarity *whatever* is implied in producing poetry, real poetry, and in any quantity—such poetry too, as, to the majority of educated and intelligent readers, shall appear quite as good as, or even better than, any other; in either sense the doctrine is false. And nevertheless, there *is* poetry which could not emanate but from a mental and physical constitution, peculiar not in the *kind* but in the *degree* of its susceptibility: a constitution which makes its possessor capable of greater happiness than mankind in general, and also of greater unhappiness; and because greater, so also more various. And such poetry, to all who know enough of nature to own it as being *in* nature, is much *more* poetry, is poetry in a far higher sense, than any other; since the common element of all poetry, that which constitutes poetry, human feeling, enters far more largely into this than into the poetry of culture. Not only because the natures which we have called poetical, really feel more, and consequently have more feeling to express; but because, the capacity of feeling being so great, feeling, when excited and not voluntarily resisted, seizes the helm of their thoughts, and the succession of ideas and images becomes the mere utterance of an emotion; not, as in other natures, the emotion a mere ornamental colouring of the thought.

Ordinary education and the ordinary course of life are constantly at work counteracting this quality of mind, and substituting habits more suitable to their own ends: if instead of *substituting* they were content to *superadd*, then there were nothing to complain of. But when will education consist, not in repressing any mental faculty or power, from the uncontrolled action of which danger is apprehended, but in training up to its proper strength the corrective and antagonist power?

In whomsoever the quality which we have described exists, and is not stifled, that person is a poet. Doubtless he is a *greater* poet in proportion as the fineness of his perceptions, whether of sense or of internal consciousness, furnishes him with an ampler supply of lovely images, the vigour and richness of his intellect with a greater abundance of moving thoughts. For it is through these thoughts and images that the feeling speaks, and through their impressiveness that it impresses itself, and finds response in other hearts; and from these media of transmitting it (contrary to the laws of physical nature) increase of intensity is reflected back upon the feeling itself. But all these it is possible to have, and not be a poet; they are mere materials, which the poet shares in common with other people. What constitutes the poet is not the imagery nor the thoughts, nor even the feelings, but the law according to which they are called up. He is a poet, not because he has ideas of any particular kind, but because the succession of his ideas is subordinate to the course of his emotions.

Many who have never acknowledged this in theory, bear testimony to it in their particular judgments. In listening to an oration, or reading a written discourse not professedly poetical, when do we begin to feel that the speaker or author is putting off the character of the orator or the prose writer, and is passing into the poet? Not when he begins to show strong feelings; *then* we merely say, he seems to feel what he says; still less when he expresses himself in imagery; *then*, unless illustration be manifestly his sole object, we are apt to say, This is affectation. It is when the feeling (instead of passing away, or, if it continue, letting the train of thoughts run on exactly as they would have done if there were no influence at work but the mere intellect) becomes itself the originator of another train of association, which expels or blends with the former: as when (to take a simple example) the ideas or objects generally, of which the person has occasion to speak for the purposes of his discourse, are spoken of in words which we spontaneously use only when in a state of excitement, and which prove that the mind is at least as much occupied by a passive state of its own feelings, as by the desire of attaining the premeditated end which the discourse has in view.*

Our judgments of authors who lay actual claim to the title of poets, follow the same principle. We believe that whenever, after a writer's meaning is fully understood, it is still matter of reasoning and discussion whether he is a poet or not, he will be found to be wanting in the characteristic peculiarity of association which we have so often adverted to. When, on the contrary, after reading or hearing one or two passages, the mind instinctively and without hesitation cries out, This is a poet, the probability is, that the passages are strongly marked with this peculiar quality. And we may add that in such case, a critic who, not having sufficient feeling to respond to the poetry, is

---

* And this, we may remark by the way, seems to point to the true theory of poetic diction; and to suggest the true answer to as much as is erroneous of Mr. Wordsworth's celebrated doctrine on that subject. For on the one hand, *all* language which is the natural expression of feeling, is really poetical, and will always be felt as such, apart from conventional associations; but on the other, whenever intellectual culture has afforded a choice between several modes of expressing the same emotion, the stronger the feeling is, the more naturally and certainly will it prefer that language which is most peculiarly appropriated to itself, and kept sacred from the contact of all more vulgar and familiar objects of contemplation. [Mill's note.]

also without sufficient philosophy to understand it though he feel it not, will be apt to pronounce, not "this is prose," but "this is exaggeration," "this is mysticism," or "this is nonsense."

Although a philosopher cannot, by culture, make himself, in the peculiar sense in which we now use the term, a poet, unless at least he have that peculiarity of nature which would probably have made poetry his earliest pursuit; a poet may always, by culture, make himself a philosopher. The poetic laws of association are by no means incompatible with the more ordinary laws; are by no means such as *must* have their course, even though a deliberate purpose require their suspension. If the peculiarities of the poetic temperament were uncontrollable in any poet, they might be supposed so in Shelley; yet how powerfully, in the Cenci, does he coerce and restrain all the characteristic qualities of his genius! what severe simplicity, in place of his usual barbaric splendour! how rigidly does he keep the feelings and the imagery in subordination to the thought!

The investigation of nature requires no habits or qualities of mind, but such as may always be acquired by industry and mental activity. Because in one state the mind may be so given up to a state of feeling, that the succession of its ideas is determined by the present enjoyment or suffering which pervades it, that is no reason but that in the calm retirement of study, when under no peculiar excitement either of the outward or of the inward sense, it may form any combinations, or pursue any trains of ideas, which are most conducive to the purposes of philosophic inquiry; and may, while in that state, form deliberate convictions, from which no excitement will afterwards make it swerve. Might we not go even further than this? We shall not pause to ask whether it be not a misunderstanding of the nature of passionate feeling to imagine that it is inconsistent with calmness, and whether they who so deem of it, do not confound the state of *desire* which unfortunately is possible to all, with the state of *fruition* which is granted only to the few. But without entering into this deeper investigation; that capacity of strong feeling, which is supposed necessarily to disturb the judgment, is also the material out of which all *motives* are made; the motives, consequently, which lead human beings to the pursuit of truth. The greater the individual's capability of happiness and of misery, the stronger interest has that individual in arriving at truth; and when once that interest is felt, an impassioned nature is sure to pursue this, as to pursue any other object, with greater ardour; for energy of character is always the offspring of strong feeling. If therefore the most impassioned natures do not ripen into the most powerful intellects, it is always from defect of culture, or something wrong in the circumstances by which the being has originally or successively been surrounded. Undoubtedly strong feelings *require* a strong intellect to carry them, as more sail requires more ballast: and when from neglect, or bad education, that strength is wanting, no wonder if the grandest and swiftest vessels make the most utter wreck.

Where, as in Milton, or, to descend to our own times, in Coleridge, a poetic nature has been united with logical and scientific culture, the peculiarity of association arising from the finer nature so perpetually alternates with the associations attainable by commoner natures trained to high perfection, that its own particular law is not so conspicuously characteristic of the result produced, as in a poet like Shelley, to whom systematic intellectual culture, in a measure proportioned to the intensity of his own nature, has been wanting. Whether the superiority will naturally be on the side of the logician-poet or of the mere poet—whether the writings of the one ought, as a whole, to be truer, and their influence more beneficent, than those of the other—is too obvious in principle to need statement: it would be absurd to doubt whether two endowments are better than one; whether truth is more certainly arrived at by two processes, verifying and correcting each other, than by one alone.

42

Unfortunately, in practice the matter is not quite so simple; there the question often is, which is least prejudicial to the intellect, uncultivation or malcultivation. For, as long as so much of education is made up of artificialities and conventionalisms, and the so-called training of the intellect consists chiefly of the mere inculcation of traditional opinions, (many of which, from the mere fact that the human intellect has not yet reached perfection, must necessarily be false) it is not always clear that the poet of acquired ideas has the advantage over him whose feeling has been his sole teacher. For, the depth and durability of wrong as well as of right impressions, is proportional to the fineness of the material; and they who have the greatest capacity of natural feeling are generally those whose artificial feelings are the strongest. Hence, doubtless, among other reasons, it is, that in an age of revolutions in opinion, the contemporary poets, those at least who deserve the name, those who have any individuality of character, if they are not before their age, are almost sure to be behind it. An observation curiously verified all over Europe in the present century. Nor let it be thought disparaging. However urgent may be the necessity for a breaking up of old modes of belief, the most strong-minded and discerning, next to those who head the movement, are generally those who bring up the rear of it. [A text on which to dilate would lead us too far from the present subject.]

ANTIQUUS.*

* This signature is only used to identify the authorship of the present article with that of a paper headed, "What is Poetry?" in a former number of the *Repository.* The writer had a reason for the title, when he first adopted it; but he has discarded it in his later articles, as giving a partial, and so far a false, notion of the spirit by which he would wish his thoughts and writings to be characterised. As Wordsworth says

> *Past* and *future* are the wings
> On whose support, harmoniously conjoined
> Moves the great spirit of human knowledge;

and though the present as often goes amiss for lack of what time and change have deprived us of, as of what they have yet to bring, a title which points only one way is unsuitable to a writer who attempts to look both ways. In future, when a signature is employed, it will be the single letter A. (Presumably Mill's note.)

# 4

# Tennyson's
# Poems

Founded by Bentham in 1824 the WESTMINSTER REVIEW was
intended to be the primary organ of expression for the utilita-
rian movement. Mill wrote for it frequently until the spring of
1828, when, partly because of his own philosophic uncertainty
and partly because of disagreement with the editor (John Bow-
ring), he severed his connection with the magazine. But in the
summer of 1834 Sir William Molesworth established a new radi-
cal review called the LONDON REVIEW, with Mill as editor. The
next year the faltering WESTMINISTER was also acquired by
Molesworth and the two journals were combined as the LONDON
AND WESTMINSTER REVIEW, under Mill's editorship.

Though it did not appear until 1835, there is evidence to
suggest that the review of Tennyson's poems was begun as a part
of the essays on poetry, and that interest in Tennyson was first
awakened by W. J. Fox. Fox had already reviewed Tennyson's
first volume with great praise in 1831, and his review of the sec-
ond volume appeared in the same issue of the MONTHLY RE-
POSITORY as Mill's first essay on poetry. There are other reasons
as well that can explain Mill's interest. He was well acquainted
with a number of Tennyson's friends, particularly Sterling and
Maurice. Perhaps most important was the widely held view that
Tennyson, as a Cambridge intellectual, was sympathetic to
utilitarian political ideas. Indeed, all of the journals which gave

44

*the 1833 volume favorable reviews were associated with the liberal side, and the most severe attack, by John Wilson Croker in the Tory* QUARTERLY, *is specifically rejected by Mill at the very beginning of his review.*

*Even though he knew that Mill's remarks were to be favorable, Tennyson attempted to forestall their appearance, and appealed to his college friend James Spedding for help.*

John Heath writes me word that Mill is going to review me in a new Magazine, to be called the *London Review*, and favourably; but it is the last thing I wish for, and I would that you or some other who may be friends of Mill would hint as much to him. *I do not wish to be dragged forward again in any shape before the reading public at present*, particularly on the score of my old poems. . . .[1]

*Considering the state of mind that this letter reveals, it is doubtful that Mill's comments had any significant effect on Tennyson's poetic practice. Sensitive in the extreme to the criticism he had received, Tennyson was, by 1835, already at work upon a full revision of his earlier work.*

*This review of Tennyson's* POEMS, CHIEFLY LYRICAL *(Effingham Wilson: 1830), and* POEMS *(Moxon: 1833) appeared in the* LONDON REVIEW I *of July 1835, pp. 402–24, now usually bound as volume XXX (1835) of the* WESTMINSTER REVIEW.

---

TOWARDS THE CLOSE of the year 1830 appeared a small volume of poems, the work of a young and unknown author, and which, with considerable faults (some of them of a bad kind), gave evidence of powers such as had not for many years been displayed by any new aspirant to the character of a poet. This first publication was followed in due time by a second, in which the faults of its predecessor were still visible, but were evidently on the point of disappearing; while the positive excellence was not only greater and more uniformly sustained, but of a higher

[1]  Hallam Tennyson, *Alfred Lord Tennyson: A Memoir* (New York, 1898), I: 145.

order. The imagination of the poet, and his reason, had alike advanced: the one had become more teeming and vigorous, while its resources had been brought more habitually and completely under the command of the other.

The notice which these poems have hitherto received from the more widely-circulated and influential organs of criticism consists, so far as we are aware, of two articles—a review of the first publication, in Blackwood's Magazine, and of the second, in the Quarterly Review.[2] The article in Blackwood, along with the usual flippancy and levity of that journal, evinced one of its better characteristics—a genuine appreciation and willing recognition of genius. It was not to be expected that a writer in "Blackwood" could accomplish a criticism on a volume of poetry, without cutting capers and exhibiting himself in postures, as Drawcansir says, "because he dare."[3] The article on Mr. Tennyson is throughout in a strain of mocking exaggeration. Some reviewers write to extol their author, others to laugh at him; this writer was desirous to do both—first to make the book appear beyond all measure contemptible, next in the highest degree admirable—putting the whole force of his mind alternately into these two purposes. If we can forgive this audacious sporting with his reader and his subjects, the critique is otherwise not without merit. The praise and blame, though shovelled out rather than measured, are thrown into the right places; the real merits and defects of the poems are pointed out with discrimination, and a fair enough impression left of the proportion between the two; and it is evident that if the same writer were to review Mr. Tennyson's second publication, his

---

[2] *Blackwood's Edinburgh Magazine* XXXI (May 1832): 721–41, by John Wilson Croker under the pen name "Christopher North." *Quarterly Review* XLIX (April, 1833): 81–96, by John Wilson Croker.

[3] Drawcansir: a character in George Villiers Duke of Buckingham's *The Rehearsal* (1671). This satirical drama was singled out by Bentham as a reason for a rejection of satire as a legitimate literary mode; it brought innocent amusements into disrepute and thus destroyed the pleasures they would otherwise have provided.

praise, instead of being about equally balanced by his censure, would be but slightly qualified by it.

Of Mr. Tennyson's two volumes, the second was the only one which fell into the hands of the Quarterly Reviewer; and his treatment of it, compared with the notice taken by Blackwood of its more juvenile predecessor, forms a contrast, characteristic of the two journals. Whatever may be in other respects our opinion of Blackwood's Magazine, it is impossible to deny to its principal writers (or writer) a certain susceptibility of sense, a geniality of temperament. Their mode of writing about works of genius is that of a person who derives much enjoyment from them, and is grateful for it. Genuine powers of mind, with whatever opinions connected, seldom fail to meet with response and recognition from these writers. The Quarterly Review, on the other hand, both under its original and under its present management, has been no less characterised by qualities directly the reverse of these. Every new claim upon its admiration, unless forced upon it by the public voice, or recommended by some party interest, it welcomes, not with a friendly extension of the hand, but with a curl of the lip: the critic (as we figure him to ourselves) taking up the book, in trusting anticipation of pleasure, not from the book, but from the contemplation of his own cleverness in making it contemptible. He has not missed the opportunity of admiring himself at the expense of Mr. Tennyson: although, as we have not heard that these poems have yet, like those of Mr. Robert Montgomery, reached the eleventh edition, nor that any apprehension is entertained of danger to the public taste from their extravagant popularity, we may well be astonished that performances so utterly worthless as this critic considers them, should have appeared to him deserving of so much attention from so superior a mind. The plan he adopts is no new one, but abundantly hacknied: he selects the few bad passages (not amounting to three pages in the whole), and such others as, by being separated from the context, may be made to look ridiculous; and, in a strain of dull irony, of which all the point consists in the ill-nature, he holds forth these as a specimen of the work. A piece of criticism, resembling, in all but their wit, the disgraceful articles in the early Numbers of the Edinburgh Review, on Wordsworth and Coleridge.

Meanwhile, these poems have been winning their way, by slow approaches, to a reputation, the exact limits and measure of which it would be hazardous at present to predict, but which, we believe, will not ultimately be inconsiderable. Desiring, so far as may depend upon us, to accelerate this progress, and also not without a desire to exhibit, to any who still have faith in the Quarterly Review, the value of its critical judgments, we propose to lay before those of our readers who are still unacquainted with the poems, such specimens as may justify the terms in which we have spoken of them—interspersing or subjoining a few remarks on the character and the present state of development of Mr. Tennyson's poetic endowment.

Of all the capacities of a poet, that which seems to have arisen earliest in Mr. Tennyson, and in which he most excels, is that of scene-painting, in the higher sense of the term: not the mere power of producing that rather vapid species of composition usually termed descriptive poetry—for there is not in these volumes one passage of pure description: but the power of *creating* scenery, in keeping with some state of human feeling; so fitted to it as to be the embodied symbol of it, and to summon up the state of feeling itself, with a force not to be surpassed by anything but reality. Our first specimen, selected from the earlier of the two volumes, will illustrate chiefly this quality of Mr. Tennyson's productions. We do not anticipate that this little poem will be equally relished at first by all lovers of poetry: and indeed if it were, its merit could be but of the humblest kind; for sentiments and imagery which can be received at once, and with equal ease, into every mind, must necessarily be

48

trite. Nevertheless, we do not hesitate to quote it at full length. The subject is Mariana, the Mariana of "Measure for Measure," living deserted and in solitude in the "moated grange." The ideas which these two words suggest, impregnated with the feelings of the supposed inhabitant, have given rise to the following picture:—[4]

> "With blackest moss the flower-pots
>     Were thickly crusted, one and all,
> The rusted nails fell from the knots
>     That held the peach to the garden-wall.
> The broken sheds looked sad and strange,
>     Unlifted was the clinking latch,
>     Weeded and worn the ancient thatch
> Upon the lonely moated grange.
>     She only said, 'My life is dreary,
>       He cometh not,' she said;
>     She said, 'I am aweary, aweary;
>       I would that I were dead!'
>
> "Her tears fell with the dews at even,
>     Her tears fell ere the dews were dried,
> She could not look on the sweet heaven,
>     Either at morn or eventide.
> After the flitting of the bats,
>     When thickest dark did trance the sky,
>     She drew her casement-curtain by,
> And glanced athwart the glooming flats.
>     She only said, 'The night is dreary,
>       He cometh not,' she said:
>     She said, 'I am aweary, aweary,
>       I would that I were dead!'
>
> "Upon the middle of the night,
>     Waking she heard the night-fowl crow:
> The cock sung out an hour ere light:
>     From the dark fen the oxen's low

[4] Mill is of course quoting from the original version of these poems. Tennyson spent much effort in revision before the appearance of *Poems* in 1842. Several poems were eliminated and many others, including "The Lady of Shalott," were extensively rewritten.

Came to her: without hope of change,
　In sleep she seemed to walk forlorn,
　Till cold winds woke the grey-eyed morn
About the lonely moated grange.
　　She only said, 'The day is dreary,
　　He cometh not,' she said;
　　She said, 'I am aweary, aweary,
　　I would that I were dead!'

"About a stone-cast from the wall
　A sluice with blackened waters slept,
And o'er it many, round and small,
　The clustered marishmosses crept.
Hard by, a poplar shook alway,
　All silver-green with gnarled bark,
　For leagues no other tree did dark
The level waste, the rounding grey.
　　She only said, 'My life is dreary,
　　He cometh not,' she said;
　　She said, 'I am aweary, aweary,
　　I would that I were dead!'

"And ever when the moon was low,
　And the shrill winds were up an' away,
In the white curtain, to and fro,
　She saw the gusty shadow sway.
But when the moon was very low,
　And wild winds bound within their cell,
　The shadow of the poplar fell
Upon her bed, across her brow.
　　She only said, 'The night is dreary
　　He cometh not,' she said;
　　She said, 'I am aweary, aweary,
　　I would that I were dead!

"All day within the dreamy house,
　The doors upon their hinges creaked,
The blue-fly sung i' the pane; the mouse
　Behind the mouldering wainscot shrieked,
Or from the crevice peered about.
　Old faces glimmered through the doors,
　Old footsteps trod the upper floors,

Old voices called her from without.
   She only said, 'My life is dreary,
     He cometh not,' she said;
   She said, 'I am aweary, aweary,
     I would that I were dead!'

"The sparrow's chirrup on the roof,
   The slow clock ticking, and the sound
Which to the wooing wind aloof
   The poplar made, did all confound
Her sense; but most she loathed the hour
   When the thickmoted sunbeam lay
   Athwart the chambers, and the day
Downsloped was westering in his bower.
   Then, said she, 'I am very dreary,
     He will not come,' she said;
   She wept, 'I am aweary, aweary,
     Oh God, that I were dead!'"

In the one peculiar and rare quality which we intended to illustrate by it, this poem appears to us to be pre-eminent. We do not, indeed, defend all the expressions in it, some of which seem to have been extorted from the author by the tyranny of rhyme; and we might find much more to say against the poem, if we insisted upon judging of it by a wrong standard. The nominal subject excites anticipations which the poem does not even attempt to fulfil. The humblest poet, who is a poet at all, could make more than is here made of the situation of a maiden abandoned by her lover. But that was not Mr. Tennyson's idea. The love-story is secondary in his mind. The words "he cometh not" are almost the only words which allude to it at all. To place ourselves at the right point of view, we must drop the conception of Shakespeare's Mariana, and retain only that of a "moated grange," and a solitary dweller within it, forgotten by mankind. And now see whether poetic imagery ever conveyed a more intense conception of such a place, or of the feelings of such an inmate. From the very first line, the rust of age and the solitude of desertion are[,] on the whole[,] picture.[5] Words surely never excited a more vivid feeling of physical and spiritual dreariness: and not dreariness alone—for that might be felt under many other circumstances of solitude—but the dreariness which speaks not merely of being far from human converse and sympathy, but of being *deserted* by it.

Our next specimen shall be of a character remote from this. It is the second of two poems, "The May Queen" and "New Year's Eve"—the one expressing the wild, overflowing spirits of a light-hearted girl, just chosen Queen of the May; the latter, the feelings of the same girl some months afterwards, when dying by a gradual decay. We regret that the opening of the latter poem must lose in our pages the effect of contrast produced by its immediately succeeding the former:—

> "If you're waking, call me early, call me early, mother dear,
> For I would see the sun rise upon the glad Newyear.
> It is the last Newyear that I shall ever see,
> Then ye may lay me low i' the mould, and think no more o'
> me.

> "To-night I saw the sun set: he set and left behind
> The good old year, the dear old time, and all my peace of
> mind;
> And the Newyear's coming up, mother, but I shall never see
> The may upon the blackthorn, the leaf upon the tree.

> "Last May we made a crown of flowers: we had a merry day;
> Beneath the hawthorn on the green they made me Queen of
> May;
> And we danced about the maypole and in the hazel-copse,
> Till Charles's wain came out above the tall white chimney-
> tops.

> "There's not a flower on all the hills: the frost is on the pane:
> I only wish to live till the snow-drops come again:
> I wish the snow could melt and the sun come out on high—
> I long to see a flower so before the day I die.

[5] Punctuation in the original is incorrect.

"The building rook will caw from the windy tall elmtree
And the tufted plover pipe along the fallow lea,
And the swallow will come back again with summer o'er the
　　wave,
But I shall lie alone, mother, within the mouldering grave.

"Upon the chancel-casement, and upon the grave o' mine,
In the early early morning the summer sun will shine,
Before the red cock crows from the farm upon the hill,
When you are warm-asleep, mother, and all the world is still.

"When the flowers come again, mother, beneath the waning
　　light,
Ye'll never see me more in the long gray fields at night;
When from the dry dark wold the summer airs blow cool,
On the oat-grass and the sword-grass, and the bulrush in the
　　pool.

"Ye'll bury me, my mother, just beneath the hawthorn shade,
And ye'll come sometimes and see me where I am lowly laid.
I shall not forget ye, mother, I shall hear ye when ye pass,
With your feet above my head in the long and pleasant grass.

"I have been wild and wayward, but ye'll forgive me now;
Ye'll kiss me, my own mother, upon my cheek and brow;
Nay—nay, ye must not weep, nor let your grief be wild,
Ye should not fret for me, mother, ye have another child.

"If I can I'll come again, mother, from out my resting place;
Though ye'll not see me, mother, I shall look upon your face;
Though I cannot speak a word, I shall hearken what ye say,
And be often—often with ye when ye think I'm far away.

"Goodnight, goodnight, when I have said goodnight for
　　evermore,
And ye see me carried out from the threshold of the door;
Don't let Effie come to see me till my grave be growing green:
She'll be a better child to you than ever I have been.

"She'll find my garden tools upon the granary floor:
Let her take 'em: they are hers: I shall never garden more:
But tell her, when I'm gone, to train the rosebush that I set,
About the parlour-window and the box of mignonette.

"Good-night, sweet mother: call me when it begins to dawn.
All night I lie awake, but I fall asleep at morn;
But I would see the sun rise upon the glad Newyear,
So, if your're waking, call me, call me early, mother dear."[6]

This poem is fitted for a more extensive popularity than any other in the two volumes. Simple, genuine pathos, arising out of the situations and feelings common to mankind generally, is of all kinds of poetic beauty that which can be most universally appreciated; and the genius implied in it is, in consequence, apt to be overrated, for it is also of all kinds that which can be most easily produced. In this poem there is not only the truest pathos, but (except in one passage*) perfect harmony and keeping.

The next poem which we shall quote is one of higher pretensions. Its length exceeds the usual dimensions of an extract. But the idea which would be given of the more perfect of Mr. Tennyson's poems, by detached passages, would be not merely an incomplete but a false idea. There is not a stanza in the following poem which can be felt or even understood as the poet intended, unless the reader's imagination and feelings are already in the state which results from the passage next preceding, or rather from all which precedes. The very breaks, which divide the story into parts, all tell.

If every one approached poetry in the spirit in which it ought to be approached, willing to feel it first and examine it afterwards, we should not premise another word. But there is a class of readers, (a class, too, on whose verdict the early success of a young poet mainly depends,) who dare not enjoy until they have first satisfied themselves that they have a warrant for enjoying; who read a poem with the critical understanding first,

---

* We allude to the second line of the second stanza. The concluding words of the line appear to us altogether out of keeping with the rest of the poem.

[6] This is the entire poem as originally published. In 1842 Tennyson added a "Conclusion" of 60 lines, which shows the speaker, having survived the winter, now ready to die in the spring.

and only when they are convinced that it is right to be delighted, are willing to give their spontaneous feelings fair play. The consequence is, that they lose the general effect, while they higgle about the details, and never place themselves in the position in which, even with their mere understandings, they can estimate the poem as a whole. For the benefit of such readers, we tell them beforehand, that this is a tale of enchantment; and that they will never enter into the spirit of it unless they surrender their imagination to the guidance of the poet, with the same easy credulity with which they would read the "Arabian Nights," or, what this story more resembles, the tales of magic of the middle ages.

Though the agency is supernatural, the scenery, as will be perceived, belongs to the actual world. No reader of any imagination will complain, the precise nature of the enchantment is left in mystery.

### THE LEGEND OF THE LADY OF SHALOTT.
#### *"Part the First.*

"On either side the river lie
Long fields of barley and of rye,
That clothe the wold, and meet the sky;
And thro' the field the road runs by
       To manytower'd Camelot.
The yellowleavèd waterlily,
The green-sheathèd daffodilly,
Tremble in the water chilly,
       Round about Shalott.

"Willows whiten, aspens shiver,
The sunbeam-showers break and quiver
In the stream that runneth ever
By the island in the river,
       Flowing down to Camelot.
Four grey walls and four grey towers
Overlook a space of flowers,
And the silent isle imbowers
       The Lady of Shalott.

"Underneath the bearded barley,
The reaper, reaping late and early,
Hears her ever chanting cheerly,
Like an angel, singing clearly,
  O'er the stream of Camelot.
Piling the sheaves in furrows airy,
Beneath the moon, the reaper weary
Listening whispers, ''Tis the fairy
  Lady of Shalott.'

"The little isle is all inrailed
With a rose-fence, and overtrailed
With roses: by the marge unhailed
The shallop flitteth silken-sailed,
  Skimming down to Camelot.
A pearl garland winds her head:
She leaneth on a velvet bed,
Full royally apparrellèd,
  The Lady of Shalott.

*"Part the Second.*

"No time has she to sport and play:
A charmed web she weaves alway,
A curse is on her, if she stay
Her weaving, either night or day,
  To look down to Camelot.
She knows not what the curse may be;
Therefore she weaveth steadily,
Therefore no other care hath she,
  The Lady of Shalott.

"She lives with little joy or fear.
Over the water, running near,
The sheepbell tinkles in her ear.
Before her hangs a mirror clear,
  Reflecting towered Camelot.
And, as the mazy web she whirls,
She sees the surly village-shurls,
And the red-cloaks of market girls,
  Pass onward from Shalott.

"Sometimes a troop of damsels glad,
An abbot or an ambling pad,
Sometimes a curly shepherd lad,
Or longhaired page, in crimson clad,
  Goes by to towered Camelot.
And sometimes thro' the mirror blue,
The knights come riding, two and two.
She hath no loyal knight and true,
  The Lady of Shalott.

"But in her web she still delights
To weave the mirror's magic sights:
For often thro' the silent nights,
A funeral, with plumes and lights
  And music, came from Camelot.
Or, when the moon was overhead,
Came two young lovers, lately wed:
'I am half-sick of shadows,' said
  The Lady of Shalott.

  *"Part the Third.*

"A bow-shot from her bower-eaves
He rode between the barley-sheaves:
The sun came dazzling thro' the leaves,
And flamed upon the brazen greaves
  Of bold Sir Launcelot.
A redcross knight for ever kneeled
To a lady in his shield,
That sparkled on the yellow field,
  Beside remote Shalott.

"The gemmy bridle glittered free,
Like to some branch of stars we see
Hung in the golden galaxy.
The bridle-bells rang merrily
  As he rode down from Camelot.
And, from his blazoned baldric slung,
A mighty silver bugle hung,
And, as he rode, his armour rung,
  Beside remote Shalott.

"All in the blue unclouded weather,
Thickjewelled shone the saddle-leather.
The helmet, and the helmet-feather,
Burned like one burning flame together,
          As he rode down from Camelot.
As often thro' the purple night,
Below the starry clusters bright,
Some bearded meteor, trailing light,
          Moves over green Shalott.

"His broad clear brow in sunlight glowed.
On burnished hooves his war-horse trode.
From underneath his helmet flowed
His coalblack curls, as on he rode,
          As he rode down from Camelot.
From the bank, and from the river,
He flashed into the crystal mirror,
'Tirra lirra, tirra lirra,'
          Sang Sir Launcelot.*

"She left the web: she left the loom:
She made three paces thro' the room:
She saw the waterflower bloom:
She saw the helmet and the plume:
          She looked down to Camelot.
Out flew the web, and floated wide,
The mirror cracked from side to side,
'The curse is come upon me,' cried
          The Lady of Shalott.

*"Part the Fourth.*

"In the stormy eastwind straining,
The pale-yellow woods were waning,
The broad stream in his banks complaining,
Heavily the low sky raining
          Over towered Camelot:
Outside the isle a shallow boat
Beneath a willow lay afloat,

---

* In this most striking passage, which we should have thought would have commanded admiration from every one who can read, all that the Quarterly Reviewer could see is, that the rhymes are incorrect!

58

Below the carven stern she wrote,
THE LADY OF SHALOTT.

"A cloudwhite crown of pearl she dight.
All raimented in snowy white
That loosely flew, (her zone in sight,
Clasped with one blinding diamond bright,)
 Her wide eyes fixed on Camelot,
Though the squally eastwind keenly
Blew, with folded arms serenely
By the water stood the queenly
 Lady of Shalott.

"With a steady, stony glance—
Like some bold seer in a trance,
Beholding all his own mischance,
Mute, with a glassy countenance—
 She looked down to Camelot.
It was the closing of the day,
She loosed the chain, and down she lay,
The broad stream bore her far away,
 The Lady of Shalott.

"As when to sailors while they roam,
By creeks and outfalls far from home,
Rising and dropping with the foam,
From dying swans wild warblings come,
 Blown shoreward; so to Camelot
Still as the boathead wound along,
The willowy hills and fields among,
They heard her chanting her deathsong,
 The Lady of Shalott.

"A longdrawn carol, mournful, holy,
She chanted loudly, chanted lowly,
Till her eyes were darkened wholly,
And her smooth face sharpened slowly*
 Turned to towered Camelot:

* This exquisite line, the egregious critic of the Quarterly distinguishes by italics as specially absurd! proving thereby what is his test of the truth of a description, even of a physical fact. He does not ask himself, Is the fact so? but, Have I ever seen the expression in the verses of any former poet of celebrity?

For ere she reached upon the tide
The first house by the waterside,
Singing in her song she died,
    The Lady of Shalott.

"Under tower and balcony,
By gardenwall and gallery,
A pale, pale corpse she floated by,
Deadcold, between the houses high,
    Dead into towered Camelot.
Knight and burgher, lord and dame,
To the plankèd wharfage came,
Below the stern they read her name,
    'The Lady of Shalott.'" *

    In powers of narrative and scene-painting combined, this poem must be ranked among the very first of its class. The delineation of outward objects, as in the greater number of Mr. Tennyson's poems, is, not picturesque, but (if we may use the term) statuesque; with brilliancy of colour superadded. The forms are not, as in painting, of unequal degrees of definiteness; the tints do not melt gradually into each other, but each individual object stands out in bold relief, with a clear decided outline. This statue-like precision and distinctness, few artists have been able to give to so essentially vague a language as that of words: but if once this difficulty be got over, scene-painting by words has a wider range than either painting or sculpture;

---

* We omit the remaining stanza, which seems to us a "lame and impotent conclusion," where no conclusion was required.[7]

[7] The 1833 version contained this final stanza:

    They crossed themselves, their stars they blest,
    Knight, minstrel, abbot, squire and guest,
    There lay a parchment on her breast,
    That puzzled more than all the rest,
        The well-fed wits at Camelot.
    "The web was woven curiously,
    The charm is broken utterly,
    Draw near and fear not—this is I,
        The Lady of Shalott."

for it can represent (as the reader must have seen in the forego-
ing poem), not only with the vividness and strength of the one,
but with the clearness and definiteness of the other, objects in
motion.[8] Along with all this, there is in the poem all that power
of making a few touches do the whole work, which excites our
admiration in Coleridge. Every line suggests so much more
than it says, that much may be left unsaid: the concentration,
which is the soul of narrative, is obtained, without the sacrifice
of reality and life. Where the march of the story requires that
the mind should pause, details are specified; where rapidity is
necessary, they are all brought before us at a flash. Except that
the versification is less exquisite, the "Lady of Shalott" is enti-
tled to a place by the side of the "Ancient Mariner," and
"Christabel."

Mr. Tennyson's two volumes contain a whole picture-
gallery of lovely women: but we are drawing near to the limits
of allowable quotation. The imagery of the following passage
from the poem of "Isabel," in the first volume, is beautifully typi-
cal of the nobler and gentler of two beings, upholding, purify-
ing, and, as far as possible, assimilating to itself the grosser and
ruder:—

> "A clear stream flowing with a muddy one,
>     Till in its onward current it absorbs
>         With swifter movement and in purer light
>             The vexed eddies of its wayward brother—
>     A leaning and upbearing parasite,
>     Clothing the stem, which else had fallen quite,
> With clustered flowerbells and ambrosial orbs
>         Of rich fruitbunches leaning on each other."

[8] The objection made above to the paintings of David occurs again here. Mill is
"romantic" in his concern for "objects in motion," that is, for narrative that represents
the flux of time. David's figures are clear but fixed in a theatrical posture. Mill's grasp
of the principle of historical relativity is one of his most decisive breaks with his
eighteenth-century heritage, and one of his greatest achievements. His essays on "The
Spirit of the Age" and on "Bentham" and "Coleridge" represent this view. Similarly
poetry is preferred that shows character in action in time, with attendant changes in
psychology.

We venture upon a long extract from what we consider the finest of these ideal portraits, the "Eleänore."[9] The reader must not, in this case, look for the definiteness of the "Lady of Shalott"; there is nothing statuesque here. The object to be represented being more vague, there is greater vagueness and dimness in the expression. The loveliness of a graceful woman, words cannot make us see, but only feel. The individual expressions in the poem, from which the following is an extract, may not always bear a minute analysis; but ought they to be subjected to it? They are mere colours in a picture; nothing in themselves, but everything as they conduce to the general result.

> "How may fullsailed verse express,
>     How may measured words adore
>         The fullflowing harmony
> Of thy swanlike stateliness,
>             Eleänore?
>         The luxuriant symmetry
> Of thy floating gracefulness,
>             Eleänore?
>     Every turn and glance of thine,
>     Every lineament divine,
>             Eleänore,
> And the steady sunset glow
>     That stays upon thee? For in thee
>         Is nothing sudden, nothing single;
>     Like two streams of incense free
>     From one censer, in one shrine
>         Thought and motion mingle,
> Mingle ever. Motions flow
> To one another, even as tho'
> They were modulated so
>     To an unheard melody,
> Which lives about thee, and a sweep
>     Of richest pauses, evermore

[9] Mill quoted from "Eleänore" to illustrate the Hellenic feeling for symmetry in his review of George Grote's *Plato and the other Companions of Sokrates* in the *Edinburgh Review* CXXIII (April 1866): 297–364.

Drawn from each other mellowdeep—
    Who may express thee, Eleänore?

"I stand before thee, Eleänore;
    I see thy beauty gradually unfold,
Daily and hourly, more and more.
I muse, as in a trance, the while
    Slowly, as from a cloud of gold.
Comes out thy deep ambrosial smile.
I muse, as in a trance, whene'er
    The languors of thy lovedeep eyes
Float on to me. I would I were
    So tranced, so rapt in ecstacies,
To stand apart, and to adore,
Gazing on thee for evermore,
Serene, imperial Eleänore!

"Sometimes, with most intensity
Gazing, I seem to see
Thought folded over thought, smiling asleep,
Slowly awakened, grow so full and deep
In thy large eyes, that, overpowered quite,
I cannot veil, or droop my sight,
But am as nothing in its light.
As though a star, in inmost heaven set,
Ev'n while we gaze on it,
Should slowly round its orb, and slowly grow
    To a full face, there like a sun remain
    Fixed—then as slowly fade again,
        And draw itself to what it was before,
        So full, so deep, so slow
        Thought seems to come and go
    In thy large eyes, imperial Eleänore.

"As thunderclouds that, hung on high
    Did roof noonday with doubt and fear,
    Floating through an evening atmosphere
Grow golden all about the sky;
In thee all passion becomes passionless,
Touched by thy spirit's mellowness,
Losing his fire and active might
    In a silent meditation,

*63*

Falling into a still delight
   And luxury of contemplation:
As waves that from the outer deep
   Roll into a quiet cove,
      There fall away, and lying still,
Having glorious dreams in sleep,
      Shadow forth the banks at will;
   Or sometimes they swell and move,
   Pressing up against the land,
      With motions of the outer sea:
      And the selfsame influence
      Controlleth all the soul and sense
Of Passion gazing upon thee.
His bowstring slackened, languid Love,
Leaning his cheek upon his hand,
   Droops both his wings, regarding thee,
   And so would languish evermore,
   Serene, imperial Eleänore."

It has for some time been the fashion, though a fashion now happily on the decline, to consider a poet as a poet, only so far as he is supposed capable of delineating the more violent passions; meaning by violent passions, states of excitement approaching to monomania, and characters predisposed to such states. The poem which follows will show how powerfully, without the slightest straining, by a few touches which do not seem to cost him an effort, Mr. Tennyson can depict such a state and such a character.

### THE SISTERS.

"We were two daughters of one race:
She was the fairest in the face:
   The wind is blowing in turret an' tree.
They were together, and she fell;
Therefore revenge became me well.
   O the Earl was fair to see!

"She died: she went to burning flame:
She mixed her ancient blood with shame.
   The wind is howling in turret an' tree.

Whole weeks and months, and early and late,
To win his love I lay in wait:
      O the Earl was fair to see!

"I made a feast; I bad him come:
I won his love, I brought him home.
      The wind is roaring in turret an' tree.
And after supper, on a bed
Upon my lap he laid his head:
      O the Earl was fair to see!

"I kissed his eyelids into rest;
His ruddy cheek upon my breast.
      The wind is raging in turret an' tree.
I hated him with the hate of hell,
But I loved his beauty passing well.
      O the Earl was fair to see!

"I rose up in the silent night:
I made my dagger sharp and bright.
      The wind is raving in turret an' tree.
As half-asleep his breath he drew,
Three times I stabbed him through and through.
      O the Earl was fair to see!

"I curled and combed his comely head,
He looked so grand when he was dead.
      The wind is blowing in turret an' tree.
I wrapped his body in the sheet
And laid him at his mother's feet.
      O the Earl was fair to see!"

The second publication contains several classical subjects treated with more or less felicity. The story of the Judgment of Paris, recited by Œnone, his deserted love, is introduced in the following stately manner:—

"There is a dale in Ida, lovelier
Than any in old Ionia, beautiful
With emerald slopes of sunny sward, that lean
Above the loud glenriver, which hath worn
A path through steepdown granite walls below,

Mantled with flowering tendriltwine. In front
The cedarshadowy valleys open wide.
Far-seen, high over all the Godbuilt wall
And many a snowycolumned range divine,
Mounted with awful sculptures—men and Gods,
The work of Gods—bright on the dark blue sky
The windy citadel of Ilion
Shone, like the crown of Troas. Hither came
Mournful Œnone, wandering forlorn
Of Paris, once her playmate. Round her neck,
Her neck all marblewhite and marblecold,
Floated her hair or seemed to float in rest;
She, leaning on a vine-entwinèd stone,
Sang to the stillness, till the mountain-shadow
Sloped downward to her seat from the upper cliff*."

The length to which our quotations have extended, and the unsatisfactoriness of short extracts, prevent us from giving any specimen of one of the finest of Mr. Tennyson's poems, the "Lotos-eaters." The subject is familiar to every reader of the Odyssey. The poem is not of such sustained merit in the execution as some of the others; but the general impression resembles an effect of climate in a landscape: we see the objects through the drowsy, relaxing, but dreamy atmosphere, and the inhabitants seem to have inhaled the like. Two lines near the commencement touch the key-note of the poem:—

"In the afternoon they came unto a land
Wherein it seemèd always afternoon."

---

* The small critic of the Quarterly finds fault with the frequent repetition, in Œnone's recital, of the following two verses:—

"O mother Ida, many-fountained Ida,
Dear mother Ida, hearken ere I die."

To return continually to the same *refrain* is, as the reader must have observed even in our extracts, a frequent practice of Mr. Tennyson, and one which, though occasionally productive of great beauty, he carries to a faulty excess. But on this occasion, if ever, it was allowable. A subject from Greek poetry surely justifies imitation of the Greek poets. Repetitions similar to this are, as everybody knows, universal among the pastoral and elegiac poets of Greece, and their Roman imitators: and this poem is both pastoral and elegiac.

The above extracts by no means afford an idea of all the
variety of beauty to be found in these volumes. But the speci-
mens we have given may, we hope, satisfy the reader, that if he
explore further for himself, his search will be rewarded. We
shall only subjoin a few remarks, tending to an estimation of
Mr. Tennyson's general character as a writer and as a poet.

There are in the character of every true poet, two elements,
for one of which he is indebted to nature, for the other to culti-
vation. What he derives from nature, is fine senses: a nervous
organization, not only adapted to make his outward impres-
sions vivid and distinct (in which, however, practice does even
more than nature), but so constituted, as to be, more easily
than common organizations, thrown, either by physical or
moral causes, into *states* of enjoyment or suffering, especially
of enjoyment: states of a certain duration; often lasting long
after the removal of the cause which produced them; and not
local, nor consciously physical, but, in so far as organic, per-
vading the entire nervous system. This peculiar kind of nervous
susceptibility seems to be the distinctive character of the poetic
temperament. It constitutes the capacity for poetry; and not
only produces, as has been shown from the known laws of the
human mind, a predisposition to the poetic associations, but
supplies the very materials out of which many of them are
formed*. What the poet will afterwards construct out of these
materials, or whether he will construct anything of value to any
one but himself, depends upon the direction given, either by
accident or design, to his habitual associations. Here, there-
fore, begins the province of culture; and, from this point up-
wards, we may lay it down as a principle, that the achievements

---

* It may be thought, perhaps, that among the gifts of nature to a poet, ought also
to be included a vivid and exuberant imagination. We believe, however, that vividness
of imagination is no further a gift of nature, than in so far as it is a natural consequence
of vivid sensations. All besides this, we incline to think, depends on habit and cultiva-
tion.

of any poet in his art will be in proportion to the growth and perfection of his thinking faculty.

Every great poet, every poet who has extensively or permanently influenced mankind, has been a great thinker;—has had a philosophy, though perhaps he did not call it by that name;—has had his mind full of thoughts, derived not merely from passive sensibility, but from trains of reflection, from observation, analysis, and generalization; however remote the sphere of his observation and meditation may have lain from the studies of the schools. Where the poetic temperament exists in its greatest degree, while the systematic culture of the intellect has been neglected, we may expect to find, what we do find in the best poems of Shelley—vivid representations of states of passive and dreamy emotion, fitted to give extreme pleasure to persons of similar organization to the poet, but not likely to be sympathized in, because not understood, by any other persons; and scarcely conducing at all to the noblest end of poetry as an intellectual pursuit, that of acting upon the desires and characters of mankind through their emotions, to raise them towards the perfection of their nature. This, like every other adaptation of means to ends, is the work of cultivated reason; and the poet's success in it will be in proportion to the intrinsic value of his thoughts, and to the command which he has acquired over the materials of his imagination, for placing those thoughts in a strong light before the intellect, and impressing them on the feelings.[10]

The poems which we have quoted from Mr. Tennyson prove incontestably that he possesses, in an eminent degree, the natural endowment of the poet—the poetic temperament. And it appears clearly, not only from a comparison of the two volumes, but of different poems in the same volume, that, with

---

[10] The best poet will be he who combines the "natural" susceptibility of the Poet of Nature with the richest cultivation of intellect. Tennyson, Mill hopes, can bring together the separate strengths of Shelley and Wordsworth.

him, the other element of poetic excellence—intellectual culture—is advancing both steadily and rapidly; that he is not destined, like so many others, to be remembered for what he might have done, rather than for what he did; that he will not remain a poet of mere temperament, but is ripening into a true artist. Mr. Tennyson may not be conscious of the wide difference in maturity of intellect, which is apparent in his various poems. Though he now writes from greater fulness and clearness of thought, it by no means follows that he has learnt to detect the absence of those qualities in some of his earlier effusions. Indeed, he himself, in one of the most beautiful poems of his first volume (though, as a work of art, very imperfect), the "Ode to Memory," confesses a parental predilection for the "first-born" of his genius. But to us it is evident, not only that his second volume differs from his first as early manhood from youth, but that the various poems in the first volume belong to different, and even distant stages of intellectual development;—distant, not perhaps in years—for a mind like Mr. Tennyson's advances rapidly—but corresponding to very different states of the intellectual powers, both in respect of their strength and of their proportions.

From the very first, like all writers of his natural gifts, he luxuriates in sensuous* imagery; his nominal subject sometimes lies buried in a heap of it. From the first, too, we see his intellect, with every successive degree of strength, struggling upwards to shape this sensuous imagery to a spiritual meaning†; to

---

\* *Sensuous*, a word revived by Coleridge, as he himself states, "from our elder classics." It is used by Milton, who, in his little tract on Education, says of poetry, as compared with rhetoric, that it is "less subtile and fine, but more simple, *sensuous*, and passionate." The word *sensual* is irretrievably diverted to another meaning; and a term seems to be required, which (without exciting any ethical associations) shall denote all things pertaining to the bodily senses, in contradistinction to things pertaining to the intellect and the mental feelings. To this use, the word *sensuous* seems as well adapted as any other which could be chosen.

† We conceive ourselves warranted, both by usage and the necessity of the case, in using the word *spiritual* as the converse of *sensuous*. It is scarcely necessary to say that we do not mean *religious*.

69

bring the materials which sense supplies, and fancy summons up, under the command of a central and controlling thought or feeling. We have seen, by the poem of "Mariana," with what success he could occasionally do this, even in the period which answers to his first volume; but that volume contains various instances in which he has attempted the same thing, and failed. Such, for example, are, in our opinion, the opening poem, "Claribel," and the verses headed "Elegiacs." In both, there is what is commonly called imagination—namely, fancy: the imagery and the melody actually haunt us; but there is no harmonizing principle in either,—no appropriateness to the spiritual elements of the scene. If the one poem had been called "A solitary Place in a Wood," and the other, "An Evening Landscape," they would not have lost, but gained. In another poem, in the same volume, called "A Dirge," and intended for a person who, when alive, had suffered from calumny—a subject which a poet of maturer powers would have made so much of, Mr. Tennyson merely glances at the topics of thought and emotion which his subject suggested, and expatiates in the mere scenery about the grave\*.

* There are instances in the volume, of far worse failures than these. Such are the two poems "The Merman" and "The Mermaid." When a poet attempts to represent to us any of the beings either of religious or of popular mythology, we expect from him, that, under the conditions prescribed by the received notion of those beings, some mode of spiritual existence will be figured, which we shall recognise as in harmony with the general laws of spirit, but exhibiting those laws in action among a new set of elements. The faculty of thus bringing home to us a coherent conception of beings unknown to our experience, not by logically *characterizing* them, but by a living *representation* of them, such as they would, in fact, *be*, if the hypothesis of their possibility could be realized—is what is meant, when anything is meant, by the words creative imagination. Mr. Tennyson not only fails in this, but makes nothing even of the sensuous elements of the scene: he does not even produce, what he in no other instance misses—a suitable representation of outward scenery. He is actually puerile.

Of the two productions (the most juvenile, we should think, of the set)—"An English War Song," and "National Song," we can only say, that unless they are meant for bitter ridicule of vulgar nationality, and of the poverty of intellect which usually accompanies it, their appearance here is unaccountable. The sonnet, "Buonaparte," in the second volume, though not so childish in manner, has still something of the same spirit which was manifested in the two just cited (if they are to be taken as serious.)[11]

[11] Unfortunately, there is little to suggest that we should not take these poems

70

Some of the smaller poems have a fault which in any but a very juvenile production would be the worst fault of all: they are altogether without meaning: none at least can be discerned in them by persons otherwise competent judges of poetry; if the author had any meaning, he has not been able to express it. Such, for instance, are the two songs on the Owl; such, also, are the verses headed "The How and the Why," in the first volume, and the lines on Today and Yesterday, in the second. If in the former of these productions Mr. Tennyson aimed at shadowing forth the vague aspirations to a knowledge beyond the reach of man—the yearnings for a solution of all questions, soluble or insoluble, which concern our nature and destiny— the impatience under the insufficiency of the human faculties to penetrate the secret of our being here, and being what we are—which are natural in a certain state of the human mind; if this was what he sought to typify, he has only proved that he knows not the feeling—that he has neither experienced it, nor realized it in imagination. The questions which a Faust calls upon earth and heaven, and all powers supernal and infernal, to resolve for him, are not the ridiculous ones which Mr. Tennyson asks himself in these verses.[12]

---

"seriously." The second stanza of "National Song" may illustrate Mill's objection:

> There is no land like England
>     Where'er the light of day be;
> There are no wives like English wives,
>     So fair and chaste as they be.
> There is no land like England,
>     Where're the light of day be;
> There are no maids like English maids,
>     So beautiful as they be.

These and other militant sonnets and exercises were dropped from the 1842 volume. "English War Song" was never reprinted; "National Song" did not appear again until 1892 in a much altered form as a song in *The Foresters*. "Buonaparte" was not included in the 1842 volume but was reprinted unchanged in 1872.

[12] Mill considers himself an expert on intellectual and "mental" crises. His objection here is the same as that made to the account of the sufferings of the speaker in *Pauline*, that these states of mind are described without having been experienced and are therefore false and unreal.

But enough of faults which the poet has almost entirely thrown off merely by the natural expansion of his intellect. We have alluded to them chiefly to show how rapidly progressive that intellect has been.* There are traces, we think, of a continuance of the same progression, throughout the second as well as the first volume.

In the art of painting a picture to the inward eye, the improvement is not so conspicuous as in other qualities; so high a degree of excellence having been already attained in the first volume. Besides the poems which we have quoted, we may refer, in that volume, to those entitled, "Recollections of the Arabian Nights," "The Dying Swan," "The Kraken," and "The Sleeping Beauty." The beautiful poems (songs they are called, but are not) "In the glooming light," and "A spirit haunts the year's last hours," are (like the "Mariana") not mere pictures, but states of emotion, embodied in sensuous imagery. From these, however, to the command over the materials of outward sense for the purpose of bodying forth states of feeling, evinced by some of the poems in the second volume, especially "The Lady of Shalott" and "The Lotos-eaters," there is a considerable distance; and Mr. Tennyson seems, as he proceeded, to have raised his aims still higher—to have aspired to render his poems not only vivid representations of spiritual states, but symbolical of spiritual truths. His longest poem, "The Palace of Art," is an attempt of this sort. As such, we do not think it wholly successful, though rich in beauties of detail; but we

* With the trifling exceptions already mentioned, the only pieces in the second volume which we could have wished omitted are, the little piece of childishness beginning "O darling room," and the verses to Christopher North, which express, in rather a common-place way, the author's resentment against a critique, which merited no resentment from him, but rather (all things considered) a directly contrary feeling.

One or two poems, of greater pretension than the above, may be considered not indeed as absolute, but as comparative failures. Among these we must place the second poem in the volume[13] (which affords to the Quarterly critic the opportunities for almost his only just criticisms); and even, notwithstanding its fine sonorous opening, the "Hesperides."

13 "Mariana in the South."

deem it of the most favourable augury, for Mr. Tennyson's future achievements, since it proves a continually increasing endeavour towards the highest excellence, and a constantly rising standard of it.

We predict, that, as Mr. Tennyson advances in general spiritual culture, these higher aims will become more and more predominant in his writings; that he will strive more and more diligently, and even without striving, will be more and more impelled by the natural tendencies of an expanding character, towards what has been described as the highest object of poetry, "to incorporate the everlasting reason of man in forms visible to his sense, and suitable to it." For the fulfilment of this exalted purpose, what we have already seen of him authorizes us to foretell with confidence, that powers of execution will not fail him; it rests with himself to see that his powers of thought may keep pace with them. To render his poetic endowment the means of giving impressiveness to important truths, he must by continual study and meditation, strengthen his intellect for the discrimination of such truths; he must see that his theory of life and the world be no chimera of the brain, but the well-grounded result of solid and mature thinking;—he must cultivate, and with no half devotion, philosophy as well as poetry.

It may not be superfluous to add, that he should guard himself against an error, to which the philosophical speculations of poets are peculiarly liable—that of embracing as truth, not the conclusions which are recommended by the strongest evidence, but those which have the most poetical appearance;— not those which arise from the deductions of impartial reason, but those which are most captivating to an imagination, biassed perhaps by education and conventional associations. That whatever philosophy he adopts will leave ample materials for poetry, he may be well assured. Whatever is comprehensive, whatever is commanding, whatever is on a great scale, is poetical. Let our philosophical system be what it may, human feel-

73

ings exist: human nature, with all its enjoyments and sufferings, its strugglings, its victories and defeats, still remain to us; and these are the materials of all poetry. Whoever, in the greatest concerns of human life, pursues truth with unbiassed feelings, and an intellect adequate to discern it, will not find that the resources of poetry are lost to him because he has learnt to use, and not abuse them. They are as open to him as they are to the sentimental weakling, who has no test of the true but the ornamental. And when he once has them under his command, he can wield them for purposes, and with a power, of which neither the dilettante nor the visionary have the slightest conception.

We will not conclude without reminding Mr. Tennyson, that if he wishes his poems to live, he has still much to do in order to perfect himself in the merely mechanical parts of his craft. In a prose-writer, great beauties bespeak forgiveness for innumerable negligences; but poems, especially short poems, attain permanent fame only by the most finished perfection in the details. In some of the most beautiful of Mr. Tennyson's productions there are awkwardnesses and feeblenesses of expression, occasionally even absurdities, to be corrected; and which generally might be corrected without impairing a single beauty. His powers of versification are not yet of the highest order. In one great secret of his art, the adaptation of the music of his verse to the character of his subject, he is far from being a master: he often seems to take his metres almost at random. But this is little to set in the balance against so much excellence; and needed not have been mentioned, except to indicate to Mr. Tennyson the points on which some of his warmest admirers see most room and most necessity for further effort on his part, if he would secure to himself the high place in our poetic literature for which so many of the qualifications are already his own.

# 5
# Poems and Romances of Alfred de Vigny

In 1836 Mill became editor of the WESTMINSTER REVIEW, and James Mill died. Both events allowed Mill to express more freely his dissent from the more orthodox Benthamism of his father, especially his own greater sympathy for literature. This broader view is apparent in the essays that date from this period—the companion essays "Coleridge" and "Bentham," and the review of Carlyle's THE FRENCH REVOLUTION—and in less-well-known articles and reviews, including "the one which contained most thought": the review of the writings of Alfred de Vigny.[1]

Mill had cultivated an interest in French politics and political philosophy since 1821. Because Mill felt that the French national character or temperament was antithetical to the English, and because he considered the political climate in France to be more open to new ideas, Mill frequently reviewed French writers in English magazines, with the object of bringing new and liberal principles and attitudes to the attention of his narrower and more conservative countrymen. In addition to being French, de Vigny was the kind of poet most easily assimilated into Mill's experientialist poetic theory. Though a poet, de Vigny was an empiricist and a man devoted to reason and its use in the cause of social reform. Furthermore, he wrote mainly of factual matters, his own military experience, and history,

[1] Mill, *Early Draft*, ed. Stillinger, p. 165.

*thus providing a center of truth verifiable by reference to the external world. Finally, de Vigny's poetry provided an opportunity for Mill to discuss the relationship that he claimed existed between the nature of poetry and the "age" in which it is written. Where both politics and poetry are taken seriously, says Mill, "each will be more or less coloured by the other"; this "close relation between an author's politics and his poetry . . . is broadly conspicuous in France." Thus while ostensibly considering poetry Mill devotes much attention to the recent political history of Europe.*

*This essay also anticipates one of Mill's later views of literature by placing more emphasis than his earlier writings had done upon the utility of a work of art as a means of bringing about social and political reform.*

*This essay appeared in the* WESTMINSTER REVIEW XXIX *(April 1838): 1–44 and in* DISSERTATIONS AND DISCUSSIONS I: *312–54.*

---

Art.—*Œuvres de Alfred de Vigny.*—Bruxelles, 1837. Consisting of—1. Souvenirs de Servitude et de Grandeur Militaire.—2. Cinq-Mars; ou, Une Conjuration sous Louis XIII.—3. Stello; ou, les Consultations du Docteur Noir.—4. Poems.—5. Le More de Venise, tragédie traduite de Shakspeare en Vers Français.—6. La Marechale d'Ancre, drame.—7. Chatterton, drame.

IN THE FRENCH MIND (the most active national mind in Europe at the present moment) one of the most active and stirring elements, and among the fullest of promise for the futurity of France and of the world, is the Royalist, or Carlist, ingredient. We are not now alluding to the attempts of M. de Genoude, and that portion of the Carlist party of which the "Gazette de France" is the organ, to effect an alliance between legitimacy and universal suffrage; nor to the eloquent anathemas hurled against all the institutions of society taken together, by a man of a far superior order, the Abbe de la Mennais, whose original fervour of Roman Catholic absolutism has given place to a no less fervour of Roman Catholic ultra-Radicalism. These things too have their importance as symptoms, and even intrinsically are not altogether without their value. But we would speak rather of the somewhat less obvious inward working, which (ever since the Revolution of 1830 annihilated the Carlist party as a power in the state) has been going on in the minds of that accomplished and even numerous portion of the educated youth of France, whose family connexions or early mental impressions ranked them with the defeated party; who had been brought up, as far as the age permitted, in the old ideas of monarchical and Catholic France; were allied by their feelings or imaginations with whatever of great and heroic those old ideas had produced in the past, had not been sullied by participation in the selfish struggles for court favour and power, of which the same ideas were the pretext in the Present—and to whom the Three Days were really the destruction of something which they had loved and revered, if not for itself, at least for the reminiscence associated with it.

These reflections present themselves naturally when we are about to speak of the writings of Alfred de Vigny, one of the earliest in date, and one of the most genuine, true-hearted and irreproachable in tendency and spirit, of the new school of French literature, termed the Romantic. It would in fact be impossible to understand M. de Vigny's writings, especially the later and better portion, or to enter sympathisingly into the peculiar feelings which pervade them, without this clue. M. de Vigny is, in poetry and art, as a greater man, M. de Tocqueville,[2] in his philosophy, a result of the influences of the age

---

[2] Mill admired de Tocqueville's studies of American democracy and had written favorable reviews in the *Westminster Review* XXXI (October 1835): 85–129 and the *Edinburgh Review* LXXII (October 1840): 1–47.

upon the mind and character trained up in opinions and feelings opposed to those of the age. Both these writers, educated in one set of views of life and society, found, when they attained manhood, another set predominant in the world they lived in, and, at length, after 1830, enthroned in its high places. The contradictions they had thus to reconcile—the doubts, and perplexities, and misgivings which they had to find the means of overcoming before they could see clearly between these cross-lights—were to them that, for want of which so many otherwise well-educated and naturally-gifted persons grow up hopelessly commonplace.[3] To go through life with a set of opinions ready made and provided for saving them the trouble of thought, was a destiny that could not be theirs. Unable to satisfy themselves with either of the conflicting formulas which were given to them for the interpretation of what lay in the world before them, they learnt to take formulas for what they were worth, and look into the world for the philosophy of it. They looked with both their eyes, and saw much there, which was neither in the creed they had been taught, nor in that which they found prevailing around them: much that the prejudices, either of Liberalism or of Royalism, amounted to a disqualification for the perception of, and which would have been hid from themselves if the atmosphere of either had surrounded them both in their youth and in their maturer years.

That this conflict between a Royalist education, and the spirit of the modern world, triumphant in July 1830, must have gone for something in giving to the speculations of a

---

[3] The concept of historical relativity applied to philosophical truths that Mill uses to explain de Vigny's situation was one of the most important differences between John Mill and his father. The idea that each age has its truths which must be superceded by the truths proper for the next age allowed Mill to accept his father's authority while rejecting many of his ideas. Mill's interest in de Vigny is a working out of the principle of historical relativity. It allows Mill to place his own views in a progressive order of history and change; to revere the past without being bound by it.

78

philosopher like M. de Tocqueville the catholic spirit and com-
prehensive range which distinguish them, most people will
readily admit. But that the same causes must have exerted an
analogous influence over a poet and artist, such as Alfred de
Vigny is in his degree; that a political revolution can have given
to the genius of a poet what principally distinguishes it, may
not appear so obvious—at least to those who, like most En-
glishmen, rarely enter into either politics or poetry with their
whole soul. Worldly advancement, or religion, are an English-
man's real interests: for politics, except in connexion with one
of those two objects, and for Art, he keeps only bye-corners of
his mind, which naturally are far apart from each other: and it
is but a minority among Englishmen who can comprehend,
that there are nations among whom Politics, or the pursuit of
social well-being and Poetry, or the love of the Beautiful and of
imaginative emotion, are passions as intense, as absorbing—
influencing as much the whole tendencies of the character,
and constituting as large a part of the objects in life of a consid-
erable portion of the cultivated classes, as either the religious
feelings, or those of worldly interest. Where both politics and
poetry, instead of being either a trade or a pastime, are taken so
completely *au serieux*, each will be more or less coloured by the
other; and that close relation between an author's politics and
his poetry, which with us is only seen, and that but faintly, in
the great poetic figures of their age, in a Shelley, a Byron, or a
Wordsworth, is broadly conspicuous in France (for example),
through the whole range of her literature.

It may be worth while to employ a moment in considering
what are the general features which, in an age of revolutions,
may be expected to distinguish a Royalist or Conservative from
a Liberal or Radical poet or imaginative writer. We are not
speaking of political poetry, of Tyrtaeus or Körner, of Corn-
Law Rhymes, or sonnets on the Vaudois or on Zaragoza; these

are rather oratory than poetry.[4] We have nothing to do with the Radical poet as the scourge of the oppressor, or with the Tory one as the inveigher against infidelity or jacobinism. They are not poets by virtue of what is negative or combative in their feelings, but by what is positive and sympathising; it is in that aspect only that we would speak of them. The pervading spirit, then, of the one, will be love of the Past; of the other, faith in the Future. The partialities of the one will be towards things established, settled, regulated; of the other, towards human free will, cramped and fettered in all directions, both for good and ill, by those establishments and regulations. Both will have a heroic sympathy with heroism, for both are poets; but the one will respond most readily to the heroism of endurance and self-control, the other to that of strength and struggle. Of the virtues and beauties of our common humanity, the one will view with most affection those which have their natural growth under the shelter of fixed habits and firmly settled opinions: local and family attachments, tranquil tastes and pleasures, those gentle and placid feelings towards man and nature, ever most easy to those upon whom is not imposed the burthen of being their own protectors and their own guides. A greater spirit of reverence, deeper humility, the virtues of abnegation and forbearance carried to a higher degree, will distinguish his favorite personages: while, as subjection to a common faith and law brings the most diverse characters to the same standard, and tends more or less to efface their differences, a certain monotony of goodness will be apparent, and a degree of

---

[4] These are examples of polemical poems written for a specific cause and aiming to arouse emotion and inspire action. Thus all are eloquence, not poetry. Tyrtaeus was a Spartan poet of the 7th century B.C., who wrote inspirational songs for soldiers. Karl Theodor Korner (1791–1813) was the author of patriotic lyrics published in 1814. Ebenezer Elliott's *Corn Law Rhymes* protested a tax on bread in 1828. The Vaudois or Waldensians were a persecuted Protestant sect on whose behalf Milton wrote the well known sonnet "Avenge O Lord Thy Slaughtered Saints." Augustina, the Maid of Sarragossa, was celebrated for her military bravery in defense of her town against the French in 1808–09 by, among others, Byron in canto I of *Childe Harold's Pilgrimage*.

distaste for *prononcé* characters, as being near allied to ill-regulated ones. The sympathies of the Radical or Movement poet will take the opposite direction. Active qualities are what he will demand rather than passive; those which fit men for making changes in circumstances which surround them, rather than for accomodating themselves to those circumstances. Sensible he must of course be of the necessity of restraints but being dissatisfied with those which exist, his dislike of established opinions and institutions turns naturally into sympathy with all things, not in themselves bad, which those opinions and institutions restrain, that is, for all natural human feelings. Free and vigorous developments of human nature, even when he cannot refuse them his disapprobation, will command his sympathy: a more marked individuality will usually be conspicuous in his creations; his heroic characters will be all armed for conflict, full of energy and strong self-will, of grand conceptions and brilliant virtues, but in habits of virtue, often below those of the Conservative school: there will not be so broad and black a line between his good and bad personages; his characters of principle will be more tolerant of his characters of mere passion. Among human affections, the Conservative poet will give the preference to those which can be invested with the character of duties; to those of which the objects are as it were marked but by the arrangements of nature, we ourselves exercising no choice: as the parental—the filial—the conjugal *after* the irrevocable union, or a solemn betrothment equivalent to it, and with due observance of all decencies, both real and conventional. The other will delight in painting the affections which choose their own objects, especially the most powerful of these, passionate love; and of that, the more vehement oftener than the more graceful aspects; will select by preference its subtlest workings, and its most unusual and unconventional forms; will show it at war with the forms and customs of society, nay even with its laws and its religion, if the laws and tenets which regulate that branch of human relations are among those which have begun to be murmured against. By the Conservative, feelings and states of mind which he disapproves will be indicated rather than painted; to lay open the morbid anatomy of human nature will appear to him contrary to good taste always, and often to morality: and inasmuch as feelings intense enough to threaten established decorums with any danger of violation will most frequently have the character of morbidness in his eyes, the representation of passion in the colours of reality will commonly be left to the Movement poet. To him, whatever exists will appear, from that alone, fit to be represented: to probe the wounds of society and humanity is part of his business, and he will neither shrink from exhibiting what is in nature, because it is morally culpable, nor because it is physically revolting. Even in their representations of inanimate nature there will be a difference. The picture most grateful and most familiar to the one will be those of a universe at peace within itself—of stability and duration—of irresistible power serenely at rest, or moving in fulfilment of the established arrangements of the universe: whatever suggests unity of design, and the harmonious co-operation of all the forces of nature towards the end intended by a Being in whom there is no variableness nor shadow of change. In the creations of the other, nature will oftener appear in the relations which it bears to the individual rather than to the scheme of the universe; there will be a larger place assigned to those of its aspects which reflect back the troubles of an unquiet soul, the impulses of a passionate, or the enjoyments of a voluptuous one; and on the whole, here too the Movement poet will extend so much more widely the bounds of the permitted, that his sources, both of effect and of permanent interest, will have a far larger range; and he will generally be more admired than the other, by all those by whom he is not actually condemned.

82

There is room in the world for poets of both these kinds; and the greatest will always partake of the nature of both. A comprehensive and catholic mind and heart will doubtless feel and exhibit all these different sympathies, each in its due proportion and degree; but what the due proportion may happen to be, is part of the larger question which every one has to ask of himself at such periods, viz. whether it were for the good of humanity at the particular era, that Conservative or Radical feeling should most predominate? For there is a perpetual antagonism between these two; and, until all things are as well ordered as they can ever be, each will require to be in a greater or less degree, tempered by the other: nor until the ordinances of law and of opinion are so framed as to give full scope to all individuality not positively noxious, and to restrain all that is noxious, will the two classes of sympathies ever be entirely reconciled.

Suppose, now, a poet of conservative sympathies, surprised by the shock of a revolution, which sweeps away the surviving symbols of what was great in the Past, and decides irrevocably the triumph of new things over the old: what will be the influence of this event on his imagination and feelings? To us it seems that they will become both sadder and wiser. He will lose that blind faith in the Past, which previously might have tempted him to fight for it with a mistaken ardour, against what is generous and worthy in the new doctrines. The fall of the objects of his reverence, will naturally, if he has an eye, open it to the perception of that in them whereby they deserved to fall. But while he is thus disenchanted of the old things, he will not have acquired that faith in the new, which animated the Radical poet. Having it not before, there is nothing in the triumph of those new things which can inspire him with it: institutions and creeds fall by their own badness, not by the goodness of that which strikes the actual blow. The destiny of mankind, therefore, will naturally appear to him in rather sombre colours; gloomy he may not be, for to be gloomy is to be morbid, but there will be everywhere a tendency to the elegiac, to the contemplative and melancholy rather than to the epic and active; his song will be a subdued and plaintive symphony, more or less melodious according to the measure of his genius, on the old theme of blasted hopes and defeated aspirations. Yet there will now be nothing partial or one-sided in his sympathies: no sense of a conflict to be maintained, of a position to be defended against assailants, will warp the impartiality of his pity—will make him feel that there are wrongs and sufferings which must be dissembled, inconsistencies which must be patched up, vanities which he must attempt to consider serious, false pretences which he must try to mistake for truths, lest he should be too little satisfied with his own cause to do his duty as a combatant for it: he will no longer feel obliged to treat all that part of human nature which rebelled against the old ideas, as if it were accursed—all those human joys and sufferings, hopes and fears, which were the strength of the new doctrines, and which the old ones did not take sufficient account of, as if they were unworthy of his sympathy. His heart will open itself freely and largely to the love of all that is loveable, to pity of all that is pitiable: every cry of suffering humanity will strike a responsive chord in his breast; whoever carries nobly his own share of the general burthen of human life, or generously helps to lighten that of another, is sure of his homage; while he has a deep fraternal charity for the erring and disappointed—for those who have aspired and fallen—who have fallen because they have aspired, because they too have felt those infinite longings for something greater than merely to live and die, which he as a poet has felt—which, as a poet, he cannot but have been conscious that he would have purchased the realization of by an even greater measure of error and suffering—and which, as a poet disenchanted, he knows too well the pain of renouncing,

84

not to feel a deep indulgence for those who are victims of their inability to make the sacrifice.

In this ideal portraiture may be seen the genuine lineaments of Alfred de Vigny. The same features may, indeed, be traced, more or less, in the greater part of the Royalist literature of young France; even in Balzac all these characteristics are distinctly visible, blended of course with his individual peculiarities, and modified by them. But M. de Vigny is the most perfect type, because he, more entirely than most others, writes from his real feelings, and not from mere play of fancy. Many a writer in France, of no creed at all, and who therefore gives himself all the latitude of a Movement poet, is a Royalist with his imagination merely, for the sake of the picturesque effect of donjons and cloisters, crusaders and troubadours. And in retaliation many a Liberal or Republican critic will stand up stiffly for the old school in literature, for the *grand siecle*, because, like him, it fetches its models from Greece or Rome; and will keep no terms with the innovators who find anything grand and poetical in the middle ages, or who fancy that barons or priests may look well in rhyme. But this is accident; and exception to the ordinary relation between political opinions and poetic tendencies. A Radical who finds his political *beau ideal* still further back in the Past than the Royalist finds his, is not the type of a Radical poet: he will more resemble the Conservative poet of ages back: less of the Movement spirit may be found in him than in many a nominal Royalist whose Royalist convictions have no very deep root. But when we would see the true character of a Royalist poet we must seek for it in one like M. de Vigny, a conservative in feeling, and not in mere fancy, and a man (as it seems to us) of a rare simplicity of heart, and freedom from egotism and self-display. The most complete exemplification of the feelings and views of things which we have described as naturally belonging to the Royalist poet of young France will be found in his writings, subsequent to the

Revolution of 1830. But we must first see him as he was before 1830, and in writings in which the qualities we have enumerated had as yet manifested themselves only in a small degree.

Count Alfred de Vigny was born on the 27th March, 1799, at Loches in Touraine, that province which has given birth to so many of the literary celebrities of France. His father was an old cavalry officer of ancient lineage, who had served in the seven years' war, and whose stories of his illustrious friends Chevert and d'Assas,[5] and of the great Frederic (who was not a little indebted even for his victories to the *prestige* he exercised over the enthusiastic imaginations of the French officers who fought against him) were the earliest nourishment of the son's childish aspirations. In the latter years of Napoleon our author was a youth at college; and he has held up to us, in the first chapter of his "Souvenirs de Servitude Militaire," the restless and roving spirit, the ardour for military glory and military adventure, the contempt of all pursuits and wishes not terminating in a Marshal's baton, which were the epidemic diseases of every French schoolboy during those years when "the beat of drum," to use his own expression, "drowned the voice of the teacher," and of which M. de Vigny confesses in all humility, that the traces in himself are not entirely effaced. On the fall of Napoleon, he entered, at sixteen, into the royal guard; accompanied the Bourbons to Ghent during the Hundred Days, and remained in the army up to 1828. Fourteen years a soldier without seeing any service (for he was not even in the Spanish campaign)—the alternation of routine duties and enforced idleness, the *ennui* of an active profession without one opportunity for action except in obscure and painful civil broils, would have driven many to find relief in dissipation; M. de Vigny found it in contemplation and solitary thought. "Those years of my life," he says, "would have been years wasted if I

---

[5] Francois de Chevert (1695–1769) and Nicholas Louis d'Assas (1733–60) were French officers who won fame during the Seven Years War.

had not employed them in attentive and persevering observation, storing up the results for future years. I owe to my military life views of human nature which could never have reached me but under a soldier's uniform. There are scenes which one can only arrive at through disgusts, which, to one not forced to endure them, would be unendurable . . . Overcome by an ennui which I had little expected in that life so ardently desired, it became a necessity for me to rescue at least my nights from the empty and tiresome bustle of a soldier's days. In those nights I enlarged in silence what knowledge I had received from our tumultuous and public studies; and thence my poems and my books."

M. de Vigny's first publications were poems, of which we shall say a few words presently, and which, whatever be the opinion formed of their absolute merit, are considered by a sober and impartial critic, M. Sainte-Beuve, as of a more completely original character than those of either Lamartine or Victor Hugo. It is no wonder, therefore, that they were but moderately successful. The first of his works which attained popularity was "Cinq-Mars, or a Conspiracy under Louis XIII," a historical romance of the school of Sir Walter Scott, then at the height of his popularity in France, and who was breathing the breath of life into the historical literature of France, and, through France, of all Europe. The reputation of this work in its native country has survived the vogue of the moment, and, as it is entirely unknown in England, we will offer to our readers a brief sketch of it.

M. de Vigny has chosen his scene at that passage of French history, which completed the transformation of the feudal monarchy of the middle ages into the despotic and courtly monarchy of Louis XIV. The iron hand of Richelieu reigning in the name of a master who both feared and hated him, but whom habit and conscious incapacity rendered his slave, had broken the remaining strength of those great lords, once powerful enough to cope single-handed with their sovereign, and several of whom, by confederating, could, to a very late period, dictate for themselves terms of capitulation. The crafty and cruel policy of the minister had mowed down all of those who, by position and personal qualities, stood pre-eminent above the rest. As for those whom, because they could not be dangerous to him, he spared, their restlessness and turbulence, surviving their power, might, during a royal minority, break out once more into impotent and passing tumults, but the next generation of them were and could be nothing but courtiers; an aristocracy still for purposes of rapine and oppression, for resistance to the despotism of the monarch they were as the feeblest of the multitude. A most necessary and salutary transformation in European society, and which, whether completed by the hands of a Richelieu or a Henry the Seventh, was, as M. de Vigny clearly sees (and perhaps no longer laments), the destined and inevitable preparation for the era of modern liberty and democracy. But the age was one of those (there are several of them in history) in which the greatest and most beneficial ends were accomplished by the basest means. It was the age of struggle between unscrupulous intellect and brute force; intellect not yet in a condition to assert its inherent right of supremacy by pure means, and no longer wielding, as in the great era of the Reformation, the noble weapon of an honest popular enthusiasm. Iago[,] prime minister, is the type of the men who crumbled into dust the feudal aristocracies of Europe. In no period were the unseen springs both of the good and the evil that was done, so exclusively the viler passions of humanity: what little of honorable or virtuous feeling might exist in high places during that era, were probably easiest found in the aristocratic faction so justly and beneficially extirpated; for in the rule of lawless force, some noble impulses are possible in the rulers at least—in that of cunning and fraud, none.

Towards the close of Richelieu's career, when the most

difficult part of his task was done, but his sinking health and the growing jealousy and fear of that master, one word of whom would even then have dismissed him into private life, made the cares of his station press heavier on him, and required a more constant and anxious watchfulness than ever; it was his practice to amuse the frivolous monarch with a perpetual succession of new favourites, who served his purpose till Louis was tired of them, or whom, if any of them proved capable of acquiring a permanent tenure of the royal favour, and of promoting other designs than his own, he well knew how to remove. The last[,] the most accomplished, and the most unfortunate of these was Henri d'Effiat, Marquis de Cinq-Mars, and of him our author has made the hero of his tale.

The story opens in this Byron-like, or Goethe-like manner:[6] "Know you that region which has been surnamed the Garden of France? that country of pure air and verdant plains, watered by a mighty river"—followed by a tasteful description of Touraine, and, in Touraine, of the chateau of Chaumont, where, "in a morning of June 1639, the bell having, at the usual hour of noon, called the family to their repast, there passed in that old dwelling things which were not usual." The household of the widowed Maréchale d'Effiat was in the commotion of preparation for the departure of her second son, Henri de Cinq-Mars to the royal camp before Perpigan; the minister's all-seeing eye having singled him out, unknown to himself, as a fit person to fill during his employer's pleasure the dangerous and now vacant post of favourite. To share the solemnities of his leave-taking there were assembled at table, besides the family, some nobles of the suite of a young princess of Mantua, whom family circumstances had caused to remain for some time under the protection of Madame d'Effiat before joining the French court; two illustrious friends of the family, M. de

---

[6] This long summary of "Cinq-Mars," extending to page 123, was not reprinted in the 1859 version.

Puy-Laurens and the celebrated Marechal de Bassompierre; and a deaf abbé, advanced in years, who turns out to be a spy of Richelieu. Bassompierre, the old companion in arms of Henri Quatre, the very soul of honour and of *bonhomie*, represents the chivalrous hero of the preceding generation. While he, with the natural open-heartedness, artfully drawn out by M. de Launay (one of the attendant noblemen,) utters his affectionate regret for the days of the great and good Henry, and his lamentations and forebodings over the jealous and artful rule of the cardinal-minister, the young Cinq-Mars is casting a last melancholy look upon the tranquil splendour of the magnificent landscape, with its azure sky, its bright green isles, its waves of limpid gold, and the white sails of the barks descending the Loire, and sighs a last farewell to quiet joys and youthful remembrances—"O Nature, beautiful Nature, adieu! Ere long my heart will not be simple enough to feel thee, and thou wilt no longer be grateful to my eyes; already consumed by a profound passion, the sound of worldly interests fills me with an unknown trouble; I must enter into this labyrinth, perhaps to perish; but for Marie's sake—" and stifling his feelings, he takes a rapid leave, and gallops off for Tour.

"The day was *triste* and the supper silent at the chateau of Chaumont. At ten in the evening the old Marshal retired to the north tower, near the gate of the castle, and on the contrary side of the river. The air was sultry: he opened the casement, and, wrapping himself in an ample robe of silk, placed a heavy lamp upon the table, and dismissed his attendant. The window looked out upon the plain, which the waning moon lighted with but an uncertain glimmer; the sky was becoming overcast, and the scene was tinged with melancholy. Reverie was no part of Bassompierre's character, yet the turn which the conversation had taken came back upon his mind, and he recalled in memory the events of his previous life; the sad changes brought by the new reign, which seemed to have breathed upon him the breath of calamity; the death of a cherished sister; the disorders of the heir of his name; the loss of his estates and favour; the recent end of his friend, the Maréchal d'Effiat, whose chamber he occupied; all these thoughts drew from him an involuntary sigh; he placed himself at the window for breath.

"At this moment he seemed to hear, in the direction of the wood, the sound of a troop of horse, but the wind rising at the same moment, made him think himself mistaken, and all sound suddenly ceasing, it passed from his memory. He watched for some time the various lights of the castle as they were successively extinguished, after winding among the embrasured windows of the staircases and flitting about the courtyards and stables; then reposing on his vast tapestry-covered fauteuil, his arm leaning on the table, he sunk into reflection, and presently taking from his bosom a medallion, suspended by a black ribbon, 'Come,' said he, 'my kind old master, converse with me as thou didst so often; forget thy court in the joyous laugh of a true friend; consult me once again on Austria and her ambition; tell me once more, inconstant knight of the *bonhomie* of thy loves and the frankness of thy inconstancies; reproach me again, heroic soldier, with outshining thee in combat—ah! why did I not so at Paris—why received I not thy fatal wound! The blessings thy reign brought to the world have perished with thee.'

"His tears dimmed the glass of the medallion, and he was effacing them by respectful kisses, when his door hastily opened, made him start, and lay his hand on his sword. *Qui va là?* he cried in a tone of surprise. His surprise was greater on recognizing M. De Launay, who advanced to him hat in hand, and said with some embarrassment, 'M. le Maréchal, it is with a heart full of grief that I am forced to inform you that the King has commanded me to arrest you. A coach awaits you at the gate, with thirty *mousquetaires* of M. the Cardinal-Duke.'

"Bassompierre was still seated, and had the medallion in his left hand, his sword in the right. He extended it disdainfully to the man, and said, 'Monsieur, I know that I have lived too long, and it was of that I was thinking. It is in the name of the great Henry that I peaceably surrender my sword to his son. Follow me.' He said this with a look of so much firmness that De Launay could not meet it, and followed him with downcast looks as if he himself had just been arrested by the noble old man."

As De Launay and his prisoner passed through a defile in a wood, the carriage was stopped by an attempt at rescue; the young Cinq-Mars, returning secretly to the chateau for a parting interview with the lady of his love, would have liberated the Marshal, had not his submissive loyalty rejected the offer of escape. They part, the one to his twelve years' captivity in the Bastille, where our history leaves him; the other to the chamber-window of the Princess Maria de Gonzague.

"It was past midnight, and the roofs and turrets of the castle formed a black mass, but just distinguishable in the extreme darkness from the clouded sky. Without dismounting, he lifted the *jalousie* of the window, and was answered by a soft low voice behind the casement, 'Is it you, M. de Cinq-Mars?' 'Alas! who else should it be, that returns like a malefactor to his parental home, without visiting his mother and bidding her again adieu? who, but I, would return to bewail the present, expecting nothing from the future?'

"The soft voice faltered, and tears accompanied the answer. 'Alas! Henri, of what do you complain? Have not I done more, far more than I ought? Is it my fault if my ill-fate has willed that a sovereign prince should be my father? Can we choose our parents, and say, I will be born a shepherdess? For two years I have warred in vain against my ill-fortune which separates us, and against you who turn me from my duty. You know it, I have wished to be thought dead—I have almost prayed for revolutions! I could have blest the blow which should have taken away my rank; I thanked God when my father was deprived of his throne. But the Court wonders, the Queen demands me, our dreams must take flight. Henri, our slumber has been too long—let us awake with courage. Think no more of these two cherished years: forget all, remember only our great resolution—have but one thought; be ambitious from—ambitious for me. . . .'

"'And must all be forgotten, Marie?' said Cinq-Mars, in a gentle tone.

"She hesitated. 'Yes—all that I have myself forgotten,' she replied. An instant after, she resumed with vivacity—

"'Yes; forget our happy days, our long evenings, and even our walks in the wood and on the lake; but remember the future; go: your father was a Marshal, be more, be Constable; Prince. Go; you are young, noble, rich, brave beloved—'

"'Forever?' asked Henri.

"'For life and eternity.'

"Cinq-Mars started with emotion, and extending his hand cried, 'I swear then, by the Virgin whose name you bear, you shall be mine, Marie, or my head shall fall on the scaffold.'

"'Heavens! what say you?' cried she, as her white hand, stretched from the casement, joined his. 'No, swear to me that your efforts shall never be criminal; that you will never forget that the King of France is your master—love him more than all, yet after her who will sacrifice everything to you, and will wait for you in suffering,' 'Adieu,' said he; 'I will go to accomplish my destiny,' and the casement closed slowly on their two hands still joined."

The light of this honest and genuine passion, illuminating the narrow and slippery paths through which the hero of our tale is conducted by his ambitious projects, bespeaks for him the truest human interest which he excites, along with the disinterested attachment of his simple and upright friend De Thou, constitutes the romance of the book.

The reader having been already brought into the midst of the age by these opening passages, is now at once introduced into its darkest recesses, by a transfer of the scene to the little town of Loudun in Poitou, during the preparation of a tragedy, familiar to readers of the "Causes Celebres," and which will be found recorded by our author with perfect fidelity: the trial and burning of Urbain Grandier, cure of Loudun, accused of having, by magical arts, caused devils to take possession of certain Ursuline nuns of that place. The characters, and almost the minutest incidents in this part of our author's narrative, are historical; the extraordinary beauty of this young priest; his talents and fervid eloquence, which excited the jealousy and hatred of his rival ecclesiastics; his unfortunate, and so far as is known, chaste attachment to the beautiful Madeleine de Brou, and the manuscript treatise against the celibacy of the clergy, written to calm her scruples, which was found among his papers; the tutoring of the nuns by Urbain's enemies, the jugglers in simulation of supernatural agency, the detection of some of these, and the failure, for a long time, of all attempts to procure a condemnation; the disgrace of imposture which fell upon the accusers, and in which Jeanne de Belfiel, the young and beautiful superior of the convent, being implicated, her uncle Laubardemont, the well-known instrument of Richelieu's judicial enormities, obtained a commission for himself to try the cause, by working upon the Cardinal's resentment for a trifling affront received from Grandier some years before, and for a lampoon of which he was lead to believe him the author. No less true to history are the horrid iniquities of this final trial: the peculiar atrocious mode in which the torture was administered to the prisoner; the appearance in court of two of the accusing nuns, smitten by remorse, to declare the whole mystery of their subordination and of their feigned convulsions; but our author

has heightened this last trait by making Jeanne de Belfiel her-
self one of these repentant false witnesses, incited originally by
the jealousy of slighted love, and driven to insanity by the un-
expected results of the machinations she had been a tool of.
One other incident is of our author's invention, at least we find
no traces of it in the history of the transaction. As the proces-
sion advanced towards the fatal pile, amidst a storm of light-
ning and rain, four priests exorcising the air which the magician
breathed, the earth which he touched, and the wood with
which he was sent to be burnt, the *lieutenant criminel* mean-
while reading aloud in a hurried manner the condemnation
and sentence; Cinq-Mars, who was among the crowd under the
portico of the church from which the procession issued, was
struck by the words, "The magician cannot utter the name of
the Saviour, and reject his image." Lactance, one of his perse-
cutors, at this moment came forth from among the *Grey Pen-
tents*, holding, with great apparent precaution and respect, an
immense iron crucifix.

"He made it approach to the lips of the sufferer, who did
certainly shrink backwards, and rallying his remaining strength,
made a gesture with his arm which made the crucifix fall from
the hands of the capuchin. 'See,' exclaimed the monk, 'he has
flung down the crucifix.' A murmur of doubtful import arose.
'Profanation!' cried the priests. The procession advanced to-
wards the pile. Meanwhile Cinq-Mars, who, from behind one
of the columns, had been an eager looker-on, perceived that
the crucifix, falling on the steps of the portico, which were
moistened by the rain, smoked and made a hissing sound.
While the crowd were looking another way he rushed forward,
laid his hand on it, and felt it burning hot. In a transport of
indignation he seized the crucifix in the folds of his mantle, ad-
vanced to Laubardemont, and striking him on the forehead,
'Villain,' cried he, 'bear the brand of this burning iron.' The

multitude heard and rushed forward. 'Arrest the madman,' exclaimed in vain the unworthy magistrate. He was himself seized by men crying, 'Justice, Justice, in the King's name.' 'We are lost,' said Lactance, 'quick to the pile.'"

The monks dragged their victim to the place of torment, while the mounted gendarmerie made head against the crowd, who pressed against them with passionate strength, drove them inch by inch into a closer circle round the pile, and at last, by one violent effort, broke and scattered them, but too late: the sacrifice was accomplished, and all that remained of Urbain was "a blackened hand, preserved from the flames by an immense iron bracelet and chain; the fingers still grasped a small ivory cross, and an image of St. Mary Magdalen," the patron saint of his beloved.

Under these sinister auspices does Cinq-Mars enter into life. His coming fate, as was doubtless intended, casts its shadow by anticipation over the very commencement of the story; we feel from the first that we are about to witness the progressive development of a dark tragedy. The author crowds with gloomy presages the outset of his hero; ominous accidents accompany his leaving the paternal home; on the night of the catastrophe of Grandier he sees, in a dream, Marie de Gonzague leading him by the hand, but pale and sad of mien, amidst the strange shouts of a mysterious multitude, up the steps of a throne, and when he reached it and turned to kiss her hand, it was the hand of the executioner. He awoke shuddering, and found the maniac Jeanne de Belfiel by his bedside, chanting over him the service for the dead, and reading in his face that he is destined to a violent death: *L'homme que tu as frappé le* [sic] *tuera.* As the mere machinery of a story all this would be childish, but it is not without its worth, even for the truth of the performance viewed as a poem or work of art; it puts the reader into the desired frame of mind, into that which is suitable

96

to the story and to the times, and does for the scene what is done by atmosphere for a picture on canvas.

We are now conducted to Narbonne on the Mediterranean, and to the cabinet of an old man, who, seated in an immense and luxurious fauteuil, surrounded by attendants busy in arranging papers but noiseless as the grave, is engaged alternately in dictating to four pages (who pass what they write to eight secretaries employed in copying round a large table) and in writing on his knee private memoranda to be slipped into the packets before sealing them with his own hand. This old man, with "an expanded forehead and a few exceedingly white hairs, large mild eyes, a pale wiry face, to which a short white beard, terminating in a point, gave that air of subtlety noticeable in all the portraits of that age; a mouth compressed, and with scarcely any lips, bordered by two grey *moustaches,* and a *royale* (a sort of ornament then fashionable, and in shape somewhat like a comma); on his head a red *calotte* or cardinal's hat; on his feet hose of purple silk; his form enveloped in a vast *robe de chambre,*" was Armand Duplessis, Cardinal de Richelieu.

A mirror suddenly betrays to this personage that his youngest page is writing a few hurried words on a slip of paper, and then hiding it under the sheet of a larger size, which the Cardinal has ordered him to fill. "Come here Monsieur Olivier."

"These words were a thunder-bolt to the poor boy, who seemed not more than sixteen years of age. He, however, stood up immediately, and placed himself before the minister, with downcast looks and dependent arms. The other pages and the secretaries took no more notice than soldiers do when one of them is struck dead by a cannon-shot.

"'What is that you are writing?' 'Monseigneur, what your Eminence is dictating to me.' 'What!' 'Monseigneur, the letter

97

to Don Juan de Braganza.' 'No evasions, Sir, you are doing
something else.' 'Monseigneur,' said the page, with tears in his
eyes, 'it was a note to one of my cousins.' 'Let me see it.'

"The page trembled all over, and was forced to lean on the
chimneypiece, while he said, in a low voice, 'It is impossible.'

"'M. le Vicomte Olivier d'Entraigues,' said the minister,
without showing the least emotion, 'you are no longer in my
service.'

"The page withdrew; he knew there was nothing more to be
said; he slipped his billet into his pocket, and opening the fold-
ing door just wide enough to make room to pass, slid through it
like a bird escaping from his cage. The minister continued the
memoranda which he was writing on his knee."

A man of sinister aspect, in the most austere dress of the
Franciscan order, appeared at the door: the attendants in-
stantly withdrew, and left Richelieu alone with his celebrated
secret agent, known by the soubriquet of *l'Eminence grise*—
Father Joseph, the capuchin friar. The conversation which fol-
lows, like all those in which the character of Richelieu is un-
folded to us, is full of dramatic power, and admirably true to
the age. The mixture of hypocrisy and frankness in the com-
munications between these two; the employer canting to his
tool, yet opening to him his real feelings also; trusting him with
all his secrets, except one, his detestation of the confident [sic]
himself, and intention to break his promises with him; while
the friar, no less treacherous to his employer, makes himself
necessary to him by playing upon his jealousies and apprehen-
sions and his colossal *amour propre*—are finely true to nature;
and no less so are the workings of such a mind as the Cardi-
nal's, when, after jesting with the lives of all the great men of
the court, he sheds tears for the fate of Strafford, a minister
abandoned by his master—when being told that the King has
'ideas which he never had before,' 'that he thinks of recalling

98

the Queen-mother from exile,' he exclaims—"Recal my enemy, recal his mother, what perfidy! That thought never came from himself—he dared not—but what said he? tell me his exact words."

"He said, publicly, and in the presence of his brother, the Duke of Orleans, 'I know that one of the first duties of a christian is to be a good son, and I shall not much longer resist the murmurs of my conscience.'

"'Christian? Conscience? those are not words of his; it is Father Caussin, it is his confessor, who betrays me. Perfidious jesuit! I must turn off that confessor, Joseph; he is an enemy of the state, I see clearly. I have been negligent these last days: I have not hastened sufficiently the arrival of this little D'Effiat, who will succeed, no doubt; he is handsome and *spirituel*, they say. What a blunder! I deserve to be turned out for it. To leave this old fox of a jesuit near the King without secret instructions, without any hostage, any pledge of his fidelity! Take a pen, Joseph, and write this for the next confessor—Father Sirmond, I think, will do.'"

And when he had done dictating his instructions to the royal confessor—

"'What tiresomeness, what interminable *ennui*! If an ambitious man saw me, he would fly to a desert. What is my dominion! A miserable reflexion of the royal power; and what toils eternally renewed, to keep that flickering light steadily upon me! For twenty years I try it in vain. There is no comprehending that man! He dares not fly me, but they steal him away from me, he slips through my fingers! What things could I not have done with his hereditary rights, if I had had them? But such a world of combinations expended only to keep my balance—what faculties have I left for my undertakings! I hold all Europe in my hand, and my destiny hangs by a hair. His cabinet of six feet square gives me more trouble to govern than the whole earth. What it is to be a prime minister! Envy me my guards, now, if you can!'"

From this time the story is full of movement and bustle: the Cardinal's levee, with all the illustrious personages of the period; then the King's camp before Perpignan, where we come into the midst of Richelieu's enemies, and the Abbé de Gondi, afterwards so well known as Cardinal de Retz, begins to flit about the scene, laughing, chattering, fighting, conspiring, the most busy and restless political intriguer of his time, having nothing ecclesiastical about him but his priest's habit, which he took by compulsion, and desires to get rid of it: the first adventure of Cinq-Mars on his arrival in the camp is to be engaged as one of his seconds, in a duel after the fashion of the time (the seconds as well as the principals fighting) with our former acquaintance De Launay. The King is then introduced; in the midst of his nobles, all disaffected to Richelieu (at least in his absence), and endeavouring, but without committing themselves, to strengthen the feeble-minded monarch in his timid half purposes of breaking with the terrible Cardinal. The King, talking quick and excitedly, and venturing an occasional jest to the nobles around him at the Cardinal's expense, tries to screw up his courage to speak the decisive word. Richelieu's enemies are in joyful expectation, and when the Cardinal enters, he sees in the face and demeanour of every courtier the forecast of his downfall: all shun him save Fabert, the commander of the troops, who with military frankness advances and addresses him—and Mazarin, the supple insinuating man of the world, who gives him a look unseen by all other eyes, expressive of the deepest respect and affliction. Richelieu takes his resolution instantly; he approaches the King, and begs permission to restore into the hands of his sovereign a power of which he had long been weary, and prepare in retirement, by prayer and meditation, for his approaching end. The King, though taken by surprise, yet shocked by some haughty expressions, and feeling that the eye of all his court are upon him, gives none of his usual signs of weakness and indecision, but coldly, and with a look of dignity, accepts the resignation. Nothing embarrassed by this unexpected stroke, the Cardinal proceeded:—

" 'The only recompense I ask for my services is, that your Majesty will deign to accept as a gift from me the Palais Cardinal!' (now Palais Royal), 'erected in Paris at my expense.'

"The King, astonished, gave a nod of consent, a murmur of surprise went through the assembled court.

" 'I also implore your Majesty to grant me the revocation of a severity of which I was the advisor, and which I, perhaps mistakenly, deemed needful for the repose of the state. There is a personage, Sire, whom, in spite of her faults towards your Majesty, and although for the good of the state I forgot too much my oldest feelings of respect and attachment, I have always loved; one who, notwithstanding her armed enterprises against your person, cannot but be dear to you; to whom, now that I am detached from the world and its interests, I feel that I owe reparation, and whom it is my parting entreaty that you will recall from her exile—Queen Mary de' Medici, your royal mother.' "

The King, who little expected this name, uttered an involuntary cry. The whole fabric of his resolution was overset; his heart was touched, he held out his hand to the Cardinal, and this moment decided the destiny of France. Soon after a courier enters with a packet, sealed with black, to be delivered into the King's own hand; it is the news of his mother's death, known to Richelieu the day before.

A duel follows, under the walls of the besieged town, ended

in the storm of an outwork by Cinq-Mars, Gondi, and others; and a battle arranged by Richelieu to amuse the King, without the intention of its leading to any result—an artifice in some danger of being discovered by the impetuous valour of Louis himself, whose feebleness (conformably to history) vanishes in the presence of the enemy; and who returns, flushed with victory, to resume his pale and melancholy look under the cold shadow of his minister. Cinq-Mars is presented to the King, taken at once into favour, and accompanies him to Paris; while the Cardinal, now apprised of his attempt to rescue Bassompierre, and of his escapade at Loudun, and discovering that he may be dangerous, lays his plans to ruin him by sending his agent Joseph (already the enemy of Cinq-Mars) to Paris, as a spy upon him. Richelieu himself remains at a distance, that his enemies may be encouraged to put themselves in his power by another, which he knows will be the last conspiracy. "Wretches," says he, as his tools, Joseph and Laubardemont, each the other's bitter enemy, leave his tent—"wretches—go, accomplish a few more of my secret designs, and then be crushed yourselves, impure instruments of my power. Soon the King will sink under the slow malady which consumes him; I shall be Regent—King—I shall have no longer to fear the caprices of his feebleness; I will destroy, without redemption, all those arrogant houses: I will pass the scythe of Tarquin over them. I will be alone above them all, Europe shall tremble—I——" he is interrupted by a gush of blood from his mouth, himself a prey to an incurable disease.

The story here passes over to years, and carries us to the Louvre, where Cinq-Mars is now Grand-Ecuyer, and the soul of a conspiracy, of which the King was tacitly the chief, to which the Queen was privy, to which the King's only brother, Gaston, Duke of Orleans, lent his name, and the Duke de Bouillon, the most powerful of the nobles, and commander of the army in Italy, his counsels. For ten days Cinq-Mars has been, not married, but affianced (by his worthy old preceptor, the Abbé Quillet, the defender of Grandier) to the Princess of Mantua, whom, constantly in attendance on the Queen, he but rarely sees in private, and that in a church and in the presence of the good Abbé, but the love of whom is the sole animating principle of his designs. The Queen, Anne of Austria, in whom our author shows us a pleasing picture of dignity and gentleness in misfortune, is not in the secret of the lovers, but, suspecting it, looks on with a melancholy interest. After an *émeute*,[7] in which the populace heap execrations on Richelieu, and shout for the King and Cinq-Mars, but which, like all the other proceedings of this unfortunate cabal, ends in nothing— the Princess speaking hopefully to the Queen of the Cardinal's loss of favour, and the King's attachment to *another*—

"The Queen smiled; she contemplated for a while in silence the innocent and open countenance of the beautiful Marie, and the look full of ingenuousness which was raised languidly towards her: she parted the dark locks which veiled that fair forehead—kissed her cheek and said: 'Thou suspectest not poor child, the sad truth, that the King loves no one, and that those who seem most in his favour are nearest to being abandoned, and flung to the man who swallows up and devours everything.'

"'Ah! good heavens, what is it you tell me!'

"'Know'st thou how many he has destroyed?' continued the Queen, in a lower voice; 'know'st thou the end of his favourites? have they told thee of the exile of Baradas, that of Saint Simon, the shame of D'Hautefort, the convent of La Fayette, the death of Chalais? All have fallen before an order from Richelieu to his master; and but for that favour, which thou mistakest for attachment, their lives would have been peaceful; his affection is deadly; they perish like the Semele on that tapestry; it dazzles while it consumes them.'

[7] A riot or disturbance.

"But the young princess was no longer in a condition to listen; her large dark eyes, veiled by tears, remained fixed on the Queen, who held her trembling hands, while her lips quivered convulsively.

"'I am very cruel, am I not Marie?' continued the Queen, in the gentlest voice, caressing her like a child who is to be coaxed into confession. 'Your heart is full my child; come, tell me what has passed between you and Cinq-Mars?'

"At these words grief forced itself a way, and, still kneeling at the Queen's feet, Marie hid her face and broke out into a deluge of tears, with infantine sobs, and violent convulsive emotions of her head and neck, as if her heart would burst. The Queen waited long for the end of this first gush of emotion, lulling her in her arms to appease her grief, and soothing her with kind expressions.

"''Ah, Madame,' cried she, 'I am very culpable towards you, but I did not think to find such a heart; I have been very wrong, I shall, perhaps, be cruelly punished for it. But alas! Madame, how could I have dared speak to you? It was not opening my heart that would have been difficult; but confessing to you that I needed that you should read in it.'"

The Queen receives her full confidence, and after some gentle reproaches, continues, as if soliloquizing:—

"'But the mischief is done, let us think of the future. Cinq-Mars is well in himself, he is brave, accomplished, profound even in his conceptions; I have observed him, he has made much way in two years, and I see that it was for Marie. He conducts himself well; he is worthy, yes, he is worthy of her in my eyes; but in the eyes of Europe, not. He must rise still higher; the Princess of Mantua must not have married less than a Prince. He must become one. As for me, I can do nothing: I am not the Queen—I am the neglected wife of the King. There is only the Cardinal, the eternal Cardinal, and he is his enemy, and perhaps this *émeute*—'

"'Alas! it is the beginning of war between them. I saw it too plainly this moment.'

"'He is lost, then!' cried the Queen, embracing Marie. 'Forgive me, my child; I am tearing your heart, but we must see all and say all now; he is lost unless he can himself overthrow that wicked man; for the King will not renounce him; force alone—'

"'He *will* overthrow him, Madame; he will if you assist him. You are the providence of France. Oh! I conjure you, protect the angel against the demon; it is your cause, that of your royal family, of your nation—'

"The Queen smiled. 'It is thy cause above all, is it not, my child; and as such will I embrace it with all my power; that power is but small, as I have told thee; but the whole of it shall be given to thee; provided, however, that this *angel* do not stoop to mortal sins,' said she with a look full of acuteness; 'I heard his name shouted this night by voices very unworthy of him.'"

The story developes itself in a narrative rapid and enchaining, crowded with incidents, and with *tableaux* full of life and character. But we see that the enterprise is not fated to succeed. Of the conspirators, Cinq-Mars alone shows any spirit or conduct; and with him it is a desperate throw for Marie or a scaffold; he knows that the poor-spirited chiefs of the conspiracy "tremble while they threaten, and are ready at the first word to make their peace by the sacrifice of him." He does what man can do, but an unseen hand plays with him from two hundred leagues off, like a cat with a mouse: the contest is with a mightier than he, and we see that he is doomed.

One scene, that of the evening rendezvous of Cinq-Mars and Marie in the church of St. Eustache, tells the story both of what precedes and what follows.

"The young and trembling Marie pushed with a timid hand the heavy door of the church; she found there Cinq-Mars, in his accustomed disguise, anxiously waiting for her. Scarcely had she recognized him, when, with a hurried step, she rushed across the church, her velvet mask over her face, and took refuge in a confessional, while Henri carefully closed the door by which she entered. Having made sure that it could not be opened from without, he followed her, to kneel, according to their custom, in the place of penitence. Arrived an hour before her, he had found the door open, the usual sign that the Abbé Quillet, his preceptor, was waiting in the accustomed place; and joyful at the good Abbé's punctuality, without going to thank him, he, in his anxiety to prevent surprise, remained at the entrance till Marie's arrival.

"The old parish church of St. Eustache would have been in total darkness but for the lamp which was always burning, and four flambeaux of yellow wax, attached to as many principal columns, over the *benitiers*,[8] throwing a ruddy light across the grey and black marbles of the deserted temple. This glimmering light scarcely penetrated into the more distant niches in the aisles of the sacred edifice. In one of the most sombre of these was the confessional, all of which, except the little dome and the wooden cross, was masked by a high iron grating, lined with thick planks. Cinq-Mars and Mary of Mantua knelt down on the two sides; they could but just see each other, and they found that, as usual, the abbé, seated between them, had been long waiting. They could see through the little grating the shadow of his *camail*. Henri d'Effiat had approached slowly; this hour was to fix the remainder of his destiny. He was about to appear, not now before his King, but before a more powerful sovereign, her for whom he had undertaken his immense enterprise. He was about to try her faith, and he trembled.

"He shook still more when his young betrothed knelt face

[8] Beniters: holy water containers.

106

to face with him; the sight of her recalled to him all the happiness he was perhaps about to lose; he dared not be the first to speak, but remained gazing, in the dim light, at that young head, on which rested all his hopes. In spite of all his love, whenever he saw her he could not help feeling a sort of terror at having undertaken so much for a girl whose passion was but a feeble reflection of his, and who, perhaps, had not appreciated all his sacrifices—his character bent, for her sake, to the compliances of a courtier; condemned to the intrigues and sufferings of ambition, to the anxious combinations, the criminal meditations, the dark and violent labours of a conspirator. Hitherto, in their secret and chaste interviews, she had heard every new step in his progress with a child-like joy, asking him with *naiveté* how soon he should be Constable, and when they should be married, as she might have asked when he would come to the tilt, and if it was fine weather. Till now he had smiled at this inexperience, so pardonable at eighteen, in a child born on a throne and bred in an atmosphere of grandeur; but he now reflected more seriously, and when, after the voices of the conspirators swearing to commence a vast war had scarcely done sounding in his ears, he heard the first words of her for whom that war had been undertaken, he feared, for the first time, that this innocence might be levity, and the childishness might extend to the heart: he resolved to penetrate it.

"'O heavens!' said she, 'how afraid I am, Henri! you make me come without carriage or guards: I tremble lest my people should see me as I leave the palace. Shall I have to hide myself much longer like a guilty person? The Queen was not pleased when I made my confession to her; if she speaks about it to me again, it will be with that severe look which you know, and which always makes me weep—I am terrified.'

"She was silent, and Cinq-Mars only answered by a deep sigh.

"'What! do you not speak to me?' said she.

"'Are those all your terrors!' answered he, bitterly.

"'Ought I to have greater ones? Oh my beloved,' said she, 'in what a tone, in what a voice you speak to me! Are you displeased because I have arrived too late?'

"'Too soon, Madame, much too soon, for the things you have to hear—for you are far, very far from them.'

"Marie wept. 'Alas! what have I done that you should call me *Madame*, and speak so harshly to me?'

"'Ah! take courage,' replied Cinq-Mars, ironically. 'You have done nothing; I alone am guilty, not against you, but for your sake.'

"'Have you done any wrong then? have you ordered the death of any one? O no, I am sure of it; you are so gentle!'

"'What!' said Cinq-Mars, 'have *you* then no part of my projects? did I misunderstand that look which you gave me in the presence of the Queen? can I no longer read in your eyes the admiration you promised to him who should dare tell all to the King? where is it gone? Was it all falsehood?'

"Her tears burst out afresh. 'I do not deserve this; if I speak not to you of this dreadful conspiracy, think you I have forgotten it? am I not unhappy enough? if you wish to see my tears, behold them. Believe me, if in our late meetings I have avoided the terrible subject, it was for fear of learning too much—have I one thought but that of your dangers? Alas, if you combat for me, have I not to maintain as cruel a struggle for you? Happier than I, you have only to contend against hatred, I against affection—the Cardinal will send armed men against you; but the Queen, the gentle Anne of Austria, employs only tenderness, caresses, and tears.'

"'Touching and invincible constraint!' said Cinq-Mars with bitterness, 'to make you accept a throne' [she was asked in marriage by the king of Poland].[9] 'I acknowledge, some efforts are

---

[9] Mill's brackets.

108

required to resist such seductions: but first, Madame, it is necessary to release you from your vows.'

"'Alas! great God, what is there then against us?'

"'God is over us, and against us,' said Henri in a severe voice. 'The King has deceived me.'

"The Abbé stirred in the confessional.

"'I had a presentiment of it,' explained Marie: 'that was the misfortune I dreaded.—Am I the cause of it?'

"He deceived me while he grasped my hand,' continued Cinq-Mars; 'he has betrayed me by means of the wretch Joseph, whom they have offered me to poignard.'[10]

"The Abbé made a gesture of horror, which half opened the door of the confessional.

"'Ah, fear nothing, Father,' said Henri, 'your pupil will never strike such blows.—Those I prepare will be heard afar off, and seen in broad daylight: but I have first a duty to perform: your child is about to immolate himself before you. Alas! I have not lived long for happiness. Your hand, which gave it to me, is now perhaps about to take it back.'

"While he said this he opened the little grating which separated him from his old preceptor, who, still silent, lowered his *camail* over his forehead.

"'Restore,' said Cinq-Mars in a less firm voice, 'restore this nuptial ring to the Duchess of Mantua; I cannot keep it, unless she gives it to me a second time, for I am no longer the same man of whom she promised to be the wife.'

"The priest took the ring hastily, and passed it through the bars of the grating on the other side; this mark of indifference surprised Cinq-Mars. 'What! Father,' said he, 'are you too changed?'

"Marie's tears had ceased, and lifting up her angelic voice,

---

[10] Poignard: a dagger; that is, a weapon not for legitimate purposes.

which awakened a gentle echo along the vaulted building, like the softest note of an organ, she said,

"'O my beloved! be no more angry with me; I understand you not; can we break what God has but just joined, and can I quit you when I know you are unhappy? If the King loves you no longer, be sure he will do you no ill, as he has done none to the cardinal, whom he never loved. Do you think all lost because he was perhaps unwilling to discard his old servant? Well, then, let us wait the return of his friendship; forget those conspirators, who terrify me. If they have no hope, I thank God for it; I shall no longer have to tremble for you. Why afflict ourselves needlessly? The Queen loves us, we are both very young, let us wait. We are united and sure of each other; the future is ours. Tell me what the King said to you at Chambord; how I followed with my eyes! how sad, to me, was that hunting party!'

"'He has betrayed me, I repeat,' answered Cinq-Mars: 'and who would have thought it, when you saw him pressing our hands, passing from his brother to me, from me to the Duke of Bouillon—when he made us inform him of the minutest particulars of the plot, inquired the very day when Richelieu was to be arrested at Lyons, fixed the place of his exile (*they* wished for his death, but I thought of my father, and begged his life!)—The king said he would himself direct everything at Perpignan; and at that very time Joseph, that foul spy, was coming out of his secret cabinet! O Marie! when I learnt this I was at first stupified. I doubted every thing, the universe seemed to totter from its foundations, when truth quitted the heart of a King. Our whole edifice was blown up; one hour longer, the conspiracy was scattered, and I lost you forever; one resource was left me, I have used it.'

"'What?' said Marie.

"'The treaty with Spain was in my hands. I have signed it.'

"'O heavens! destroy it.'

"'It is sent.'

*110*

"'Who bears it?'

"'Fontrailles.'

"'Recal him!'

"'He must by this time have got beyond Oleron, in passing the Pyrenees,' said Cinq-Mars, rising. 'All is ready at Madrid, at Sedan; armies are waiting me, Marie; armies! and Richelieu is in the midst of them. He totters, there needs but one blow to overthrow him, and you are united to me forever, to Cinq-Mars triumphant!'

"'To Cinq-Mars a rebel!' said she, with a groan.

"'A rebel, then, but at least no longer a favourite. A rebel, a criminal, worthy of the scaffold, I know it,' cried the impassioned young man, falling again on his knees—'but a rebel for love, a rebel for you, whom my sword shall make mine for ever!'

"'Alas!' said she, 'a sword dipped in your country's blood, is it not a poignard?'

"'For pity's sake, Marie! let kings desert me, let warriors abandon me, I shall but stand the firmer; but one word from you would fling me prostrate. Besides, the time for reflection is past for me; yes, I am a criminal, and therefore do I hesitate to think myself still worthy of you. Renounce me, Marie, take back this ring.'

"'I cannot,' she said: 'whatever you are, I am your wife.'

"'You hear, Father,' said Cinq-Mars, transported with happiness: 'your blessing on this second union, it is that of sacrifice, more glorious still than that of love. Make her mine, mine till death!'

"Without answering, the Abbé opened the door of the confessional, ran hastily out, and had left the church before Cinq-Mars could rise and follow.

"'Whither go you? what mean you?' he cried. But no one answered, nor came.

"'In heaven's name do not cry out,' said Marie, [']or I am

*111*

lost; he must have heard some one move in the church.'

"But D'Effiat, in alarm, rushed, without answering, across the church, to a door which he found closed. Drawing his sword he made the tour of the building, and arriving at the entrance, supposed to be guarded by Grandchamp (his servant), called to him and listened."

They found the old Abbé, his preceptor, alone in the snow, his head uncovered, himself bound and gagged. The man who had taken his place in the confessional was Father Joseph. "Fly," exclaimed Marie, "or you are lost!"

The sequel may be abridged. Marie de Gonzague verified too well the misgivings of Cinq-Mars. The Queen, who was interested for her, not for him, and to whom Cinq-Mars is now nothing but "un petit ambitieux qui s'est perdu," uses all her efforts, not in vain, to turn the thoughts of the weak minded girl into another channel; and at the moment when Cinq-Mars, at the camp of Pepignan, is about to fire the pistol-shot which is the signal for the insurrection, he receives the following letter:—

"'Monsieur le Marques de Cinq-Mars,

"'I write this to conjure you to restore to her duty our beloved adopted daughter, the Princess Marie de Gonzague, whom your affection alone withholds from the throne of Poland, which is offered to her. I have sounded her soul; she is very young as yet, and I have reason to believe that she would accept the crown with less of effort and of grief than you perhaps believe.

"'It is for her that you have undertaken a war which will fill with fire and slaughter my dear and noble kingdom of France; I implore you to act with the honor of a nobleman, and generously release the Duchess of Mantua from the promises she may have made you, thus restoring peace to her heart and tranquillity to our dear country.

*112*

"'The Queen, who throws herself at your feet if it be neces-
sary—

'ANNE OF AUSTRIA.'

"Cinq-Mars replaced calmly the pistol on the table; his first
movement had been to turn it against himself; but he laid it
down, and seizing a pencil wrote on the back of the same let-
ter:—

"'Madame,

"'Marie de Gonzague, being my wife, can only be Queen of
Poland after my death; I am dying.

'CINQ-MARS.'

"And as if not to give himself a moment of reflection, thrust-
ing it into the hand of the messenger, 'To horse, to horse,' he
cried, in a furious voice: 'if thou remainest an instant longer
thou art dead.'

"The messenger gone, he re-entered.—Along with his
friend, he stood still for an instant, but pale, his eyes fixed, and
gazing on the earth like a madman. He felt himself tottering.

"'De Thou!' cried he.

"'What would you have, friend, dear friend! I am near you;
you have been grand, noble, sublime!'

"'De Thou!' he cried again in a terrible voice; and fell with
his face to the ground like a tree uprooted by the tempest."

He countermands the insurrection, sends passports to all
the conspirators, and goes to deliver himself up, with his faith-
ful and innocent friend De Thou, who, disapproving the con-
spiracy, had entered into it from love of him, and to watch over
his safety; and now joins him in surrendering himself, resolved
to die with him. Had the insurrection proceeded he would have
found, instead of the whole army, a few companies only faith-
ful to him, the rest had Richelieu's permission to give a simu-
lated obedience: the Duke of Boullion had already been ar-
rested at the head of his troops, the King's brother had made

his peace by abject submission, and the intercepted treaty was in Richelieu's hands, to be shown to the King, to extort from him the death of Cinq-Mars. An admirable scene follows. Louis holds out long. At length Richelieu leaves him among masses of papers, and secretaries of state in attendance, to try his hand at governing. The first half hour's difficulties throw the unfortunate monarch into despair. He recals the Cardinal; says to him "Reign," and almost dead with suffering, signs the death-warrant of Cinq-Mars and De Thou.

The friar Joseph visits them in their prison, the castle of Pierre-Encise near Lyons—offers them escape and to poison the Cardinal, if Cinq-Mars will promise him protection and promotion when restored to the King's favour, the offer is heroically refused. They are tried in prison by Laubardemont, that the prophecy may be fulfilled, *l'homme que tu as frappé te tuera*. In fulfilment of Grandier's dying curse, Laubardemont himself perishes the same day, being employed first to try his accomplices in that catastrophe, whose time like his own is now come, and immediately after precipitated along with them through a trap-door into the Saone. Cinq-Mars and De Thou are led out for execution. The conspirators from the camp at Perpignan, instead of making their escape, had come in disguise to Lyons, to rescue their two friends by a *coup de main*; all is arranged, they have contrived to inform the prisoners, near every soldier there is a conspirator prepared to cut him down at the expected signal; when Cinq-Mars, in passing to the scaffold, gives the sign by putting his hat on his head, he is to be free. But he no longer desires to live: he passes, flings his hat away from him, and his head falls.

Such in 'Cinq-Mars, or a conspiracy under Louis XIII'—a work not free from the fault, so far as it is a fault, most common in the romantic literature of young France; it partakes somewhat of the "Literature of Despair;" it too much resembles M. Eugene Sue's novels, in which every villain dies honoured and prosperous at a good old age, after every innocent person in the tale has been crushed and exterminated by him without pity or remorse—through which the mocking laugh of a chorus of demons seems to ring in our ears that the world is delivered over to the evil spirit, and that man is his creature and his prey. But such is not the character of M. de Vigny's writings, and the resemblance in this single instance is only casual. Still, as a mere work of art, if the end of art be, as conceived by the ancients and by the German writers, the production of the intrinsically beautiful, Cinq-Mars cannot be commended. A story in which the odious and the contemptible in man and life act so predominant a part, which excites our scorn or our hatred so much more than our pity—comes within a far other category than that of the Beautiful, and can be justified on no canons of taste of which that is the end. But it is not possible for the present generation of France to restrict the purposes of art within this limit. They are too much in earnest. They take life too much *au serieux*. It may be possible (what some of his most enthusiastic admirers say of Goethe) that a thoroughly earnest mind may struggle upwards through the region of clouds and storms to an untroubled summit, where all other good sympathies and aspirations confound themselves in a serene love and culture of the calmly beautiful—looking down upon the woes and struggles of perplexed humanity with as calm a gaze (though with a more helping arm), as that of him who is most placidly indifferent to human weal. But however this may be, the great majority of persons in earnest will remain always in the intermediate region: will feel themselves more or less militant in this world—having something to pursue, in it, different from the Beautiful, different from their own mental tranquillity and health, and which they will pursue, if they have the gifts of an artist, by all the resources of art, whatever becomes of canons of criticism, and beauty in the abstract. The writers and readers of works of imagination in France have the desire of amusement as much as English readers, the sense of the beautiful generally much more; but they have also, very generally, a thirst for something which shall address itself to their real-life feelings, and not to those of imagination merely—which shall give them an idea or a sentiment connected with the actual world. And if a story or a poem is *possessed* by an idea, if it powerfully exhibits some form of real life, or some conception respecting human nature or society which may tend to consequences, not only is it not necessarily expected to represent abstract beauty, but it is pardoned for exhibiting even hideousness. These considerations should enable us to understand and tolerate such works as *Le Père Goriot*, of Balzac, or *Leoni* of George Sand, and to understand, though we do not tolerate, such as the *Antony* or *Richard Darlington* of Alexandre Dumas.

Now, among the ideas with which French literature has been *possessed* for the last ten years, is that of realizing, and bringing home to the imagination, the history and spirit of past ages. Sir Walter Scott, having no object but to please, and having readers who only sought to be pleased, would not have told the story of Richlieu and of Cinq-Mars without greatly softening the colouring; and the picture would have been more agreeable than M. de Vigny's, but it would not have been so true to the age. M. de Vigny preferred the truer to the more pleasing, and *his* readers have sanctioned the preference.

Even according to this view of its object the work has obvious defects. The characters of some of the subordinate personages, Friar Joseph, for instance, are even more revolting than the truth of history requires. De Thou, the pious and studious man of retirement, cast out into storms for which he was never meant—the only character of principle in the tale, yet who sacrifices principle as well as life to romantic friendship—is but coldly represented; his goodness is too simple, his attachment too instinctive, too doglike, and so much intensity of friendship

*116*

is not sufficiently accounted for; Balzac would have managed these things better. The author also crowds his story too much with characters; he cannot bear that any celebrated personage whom the age affords should be passed over, and consequently introduces many who ought not to be drawn at all unless they could be drawn truly, and on whom he has not been able to employ the same accurate study as he has on his principal characters. His Richelieu and his Louis the XIIIth are admirable, for these are historical figures which he has taken the trouble to understand; but he can know nothing of Milton, whom he introduces, on his way from Italy, reading his 'Paradise Lost' not written till twenty years after, to Corneille, Descartes, and a crowd of other poets, wits and philosophers, in the saloon of the celebrated courteszan, Marion Delorme! But these are minor blemishes. As a specimen of Art employed in embodying the character of an age, there are few works superior to 'Cinq-Mars:' the spirit of the age penetrates every nook and corner of it; the same atmosphere which hangs over the personages of the story hangs over us; we feel the eye of the omnipresent Richelieu upon us, and the influences of France in its Catholic and aristocratic days, of ardent, pleasure-loving, laughter-loving, and danger-loving France, all around us. To this merit is to be added, what our extracts sufficiently testify, that the representations of feelings are always simple and graceful; the author has not, like so many inferior writers, supplied by the easy resource of mere exaggeration of colouring, the incapacity to show us anything subtle or profound, any trait we knew not before, in the workings of passion in the human heart. On the whole, 'Cinq-Mars' is admirable as a first production of its kind, but altogether of an inferior order to its successors, the *Grandeur et Servitude Militaires*, and *Stello*; to which we proceed.

Of M. de Vigny's prose works, 'Cinq-Mars' alone was written previous to the revolution of 1830; and although the Carlist

tendency of the author's political opinions is manifest through-
out—indeed the book is one long protest against the levelling
of the feudal aristocracy—it does not, nor does any part of the
Carlist literature of the last twenty years, entirely answer to our
description of the Conservative school of poetry and romance.
To find a real Conservative literature in France one must look
earlier than the first revolution, as, to study the final transfor-
mation of that literature, one must descend below the last. One
must distinguish three periods, Conservatism triumphant, Con-
servatism militant, Conservatism vanquished. The first is rep-
resented by Racine, Fenelon, and Voltaire in his tragedies, be-
fore he quitted the paths of his predecessors. Jean Jacques
Rousseau is the father and founder of the Movement literature
of France, and Madame de Stael its second great apostle: in
them first the revolt of the modern mind against the social ar-
rangements and doctrines which had descended from of old,
spoke with the inspired voice of genius. What Voltaire did, with
all his infidelity, was but child's play compared with these two.
At the head of the literature of Conservatism in its second or
militant period, stands Chateaubriand—a man whose name
marks one of the turning points in the literary history of his
country: a conservative poet to the inmost core—rootedly feu-
dal and Catholic—whose genius burst into life during the tem-
pest of a revolution which hurled down from their pedestals all his
objects of reverence; which saddened his imagination, modified
(without impairing) his Conservatism by the addition of its mul-
tiplex experiences, and made the world to him too full of disor-
der and gloom, too much a world without harmony, and ill at
ease, to allow of his exhibiting the pure untroubled spirit of
Conservative poetry as we see it exemplified in Southey, or still
more in Wordsworth. To this literature of Conservatism dis-
couraged but not yet disenchanted, still hopeful and striving to
set up again its old idols, 'Cinq-Mars' belongs. From the final
and hopeless overthrow of the old order of society in July 1830,

118

begins the era of Conservatism disenchanted—Conservatism which is already in the past tense—which for practical purposes is abandoned—and only contributes its share as all past associations and experiences do, toward shaping and colouring the individual's impressions of the present.

This is the character which pervades the two principal of M. de Vigny's more recent works, the 'Servitude et Grandeur Militaires,' and 'Stello.' He has lost his faith in Royalism, and in the system of opinions connected with it. His eyes are opened to all the iniquities and hypocrisies of the state of society which is passing away. But he cannot take up with any of the systems of politics, and of either irreligious or religious philosophy, which profess to lay open the mystery of what is to follow, and to guarantee that the new order of society will not have its own iniquities and hypocrisies of as dark a kind. He has no faith in any systems, none in man's power of prophecy; nor is he sure that the new tendencies of society, take them for all in all, have more to satisfy the wants of a thoughtful and loving spirit, than the old had; at all events not so much more, as to make the condition of human nature a cheerful subject to him. He looks upon life and sees most things crooked, and (saving whatever assurance his religious impressions may yield to him that in some unknown way all things must be working for good) sees not how they shall be made straight. This is not a happy state of mind, but it is not an unfavourable one to poetry. If the worst forms of it produce a "Literature of Despair," the better are seen in a writer like M. de Vigny—who having now no formulas to save the credit of, looks life steadily in the face— applies himself to understanding whatever of evil, and of heroic struggle with evil, it presents to his individual experience—and gives forth his pictures of both, with deep feeling, but with the calmness of one who has no point to carry, no quarrel to maintain over and above the "general one of every son of Adam with his lot here below."

M. de Vigny has been a soldier, and he has been, and is, a poet: the situation and feelings of a soldier (especially a soldier not in active service), and, so far as the measure of his genius admits, those of a poet, are what he is best acquainted with, and what, therefore, as a man of earnest mind, not now taking anything upon trust, it was most natural he should attempt to delineate. The 'Souvenirs Militaires' are the embodiment of the author's experience in the one capacity, 'Stello' in the other. Each consists of three touching and beautifully told stories, founded on fact—in which the life and position of a soldier in modern times, and of a poet at all times, in their relation to society, are shadowed out. In relation to society, chiefly; for that is the prominent feature in all the speculations of the French mind; and thence it is that their poetry is so much shallower than ours, and their works of fiction so much deeper; that, of the metaphysics of every mode of feeling and thinking, so little is to be learnt from them, and of its social influences so much.

The soldier, and the poet, appear to M. De Vigny alike misplaced, alike ill at ease, in the present condition of human life. In the soldier he sees a human being set apart for a profession doomed to extinction and doomed consequently, in the interval, to a continual decrease of dignity and of the sympathies of mankind. War he sees drawing to a close; compromises and diplomatic arrangements now terminate the differences among civilized nations; the army is reduced more and more to mere parade, or the functions of a police; called out, from time to time, to shed its own blood and that of malcontent fellow-citizens in tumults where much popular hatred is to be earned, but no glory; disliked by tax-payers for its burthensomeness; looked down upon by the industrious for its enforced idleness; its employers themselves always in dread of its numbers, and jealous of its restlessness, which, in a soldier, is but the impatience of a man who is useless and nobody, for a chance of being useful and something. The soldier thus remains with all the burthens, all the irksome restraints of his condition, aggravated, but without the hopes which lighted it up, the excitements which gave it zest. Those alone, says M. de Vigny, who have been soldiers, know what servitude is. To the soldier alone is obedience, passive and active, the law of his life, the law of every day and of every moment; obedience, not stopping at sacrifice, nor even at crime. In him alone is the abnegation of his self-will, of his liberty of independent action, absolute and unreserved; the grand distinction of humanity, the responsibility of the individual as a moral agent, being made over, once for all, to superior authority. The type of human nature which these circumstances create well deserves the study of the artist and the philosopher. M. de Vigny has deeply meditated upon it. He has drawn with delicacy and profundity that mixture of Spartan and stoical impassibility with child-like *insouciance* and *bonhomie*, which is the result, on the one hand, of a life of painful and difficult obedience to discipline—on the other, of a conscience freed from concern or accountability for the quality of the actions of which that life is made up. On the means by which the moral position of the soldier might be raised, and his hardships alleviated, M. de Vigny has views worthy of the consideration of him who is yet to come—the statesman who has care and leisure for plans of social amelioration unconnected with party contests and the cry of the hour. His stories, full of melancholy beauty, will carry into thousands of minds and hearts which would otherwise have been unvisited by it, a conception of a soldier's trials and a soldier's virtues in times which, like ours, are not those of martial glory.

The first of these tales at least, if not all three, if the author's words are to be taken literally, is an unvarnished fact. But familiar as the modern French romance writers have made us with the artifice of assimilating their fictions, for the sake of artistical reality, to actual recollections, we dare not trust these appearances; and we must needs suppose that, though suggested by facts, the stories are indebted to M. de Vigny's invention not only for their details, but for some of their main circumstances. If he was so fortunate as to meet with facts which, related as they actually occured, served so perfectly as these do his purposes of illustration, he would hardly have left any possibility of doubt as to their authenticity. He must know the infinite distance, as to power of influencing the mind, between the best contrived and most probable fiction, and the smallest fact.

The first tale, 'Laurette, ou Le Cachet Rouge,' is the story of an old *chef de bataillon* (an intermediate grade between captain and major), whom the author, when following Louis XVIII, in the retreat to Ghent, overtook on his march. This old man was leading along the miry road, on a day of pelting rain, a shabby mule drawing "a little wooden cart covered over with three hoops and a piece of black oil-cloth, and resembling a cradle on a pair of wheels." On duty he was following the King as far as the frontier, and on duty he was about to return from thence to his regiment to fight *against* the King at Waterloo. He had begun life at sea and had been taken from the merchant service to command a brig of war, when the navy, like the army, was left without officers by the emigration. In 1797, under the government of the Directory, he weighed anchor for Cayenne, with sixty soldiers and a prisoner, one of those whom the *coup d'ètat* of the 18th Fructidor had consigned to deportation. Along with this prisoner, whom he was ordered to treat with respect, he received a packet "with three red seals, the middle one of enormous size," not to be opened till the vessel reached one degree north of the line. As he was nailing up this packet, the possession of which made him uncomfortable, in a nook of his cabin, safe and in sight, his prisoner a mere youth, entered, holding by the hand a beautiful girl of seventeen. His offence, it appeared, was a newspaper article: he had "trusted in their

*122*

liberty of the press," had stung the Directory, and, only four days after his marriage, he was seized, tried, and received sentence of death, commuted for deportation to Cayenne, whither his young wife determined on accompanying him. We will not trust ourselves to translate any of the scenes which exhibit these two: a Marryat would be required to find a style for rendering the sailor-like *naiveté* of the honest officer's recital. A more exquisite picture we have never seen of innocence and ingenuousness, true warm-hearted affection, and youthful bouyancy of spirits breaking out from under the load of care and sorrow which had been laid so early and so suddenly on their young heads. They won the good-natured captain's heart: he had no family and no ties; he offered, on arriving at Cayenne, to settle there with his little savings and adopt them as his children. On reaching the prescribed latitude he broke the fatal seal, and shuddered at beholding the sentence of death, and an order for immediate execution. After a terrible internal struggle, military discipline prevailed: he did as was commanded him, and "that moment," says he, "has lasted for me to the present time; as long as I live I shall drag it after me as a galley slave drags his chain." Laurette became an incurable idiot. "I felt something in me which said—remain with her to the end of thy days and protect her." Her mother was dead; her relations wished to put her into a madhouse; "I turned my back upon them and kept her with me." Taking a disgust to the sea, he exchanged into the army; the unhappy girl was with him in all Napoleon's campaigns even in the retreat from Russia, tended by him like a daughter, and when the author overtook him he was conducting her in the cart with its three hoops and its canvas cover. The author shows her to us—a picture not inferior to Sterne's Maria, and which will live as long: to detach it from the rest of the story would be unjust to the author. M. de Vigny parted from the old *chef de bataillon* at the frontier, and learned, long after, that he perished at Waterloo; she, left

123

alone, and consigned to a madhouse, died in three days.

'La Veillee de Vincennes' is a less tragical story: the life and destiny of an old adjutant of artillery, with whom the author, an officer in the guards, then in garrison at Vincennes, made acquaintance in the court yard of the fortress, the evening previous to a general review and inspection. The old adjutant, who was in charge of the powder, was anxiously casting up long columns of figures, feeling himself eternally disgraced if there should be found on the morrow the most trifling inaccuracy in his books; and regreting the impossibility, from the late hour, of giving another glance that night at the contents of the powder magazine. The soldiers of the guard, who were not merely the *élite* of the army, but the *élite* of the *élite*, "thought themselves," says our author, "dishonoured by the most insignificant fault. 'Go, you are puritans of honour, all of you,' said I tapping him on the shoulder. He bowed, and withdrew towards the barracks where he was quartered; then, with an innocence of manners peculiar to the honest fact of soldiers, he returned with a handful of hemp-seed for a hen who was bringing up her twelve chickens under the old bronze cannon on which we were seated." This hen, the delight of her master and the pet of the soldiers, could not endure any person not in uniform. At a late hour that night the author caught the sound of music from an open window: he approached; the voices were those of the old adjutant, his daughter, and a young non-commissioned officer of artillery, her intended husband; they saw him, and invited him in, and we owe to this evening a charming description of the simple, innocent interior of this little family, and their simple history. The old soldier was the orphan child of a villager of Montreuil, near Versailles; brought up, and taught music and gardening, by the cure of his village. At sixteen, a word sportively dropped by Marie Antoinette when, alone with the Princess de Lamballe, she met him and his pretty playmate Pierrette in the park of Montreuil, made him enlist for a sol-

124

dier, hoping to be made a serjeant and to marry Pierrette. The latter wish was in time accomplished through the benevolence of Marie Antoinette, who, finding him resolute not to owe the attainment of his wishes to the bounty of a patron, herself taught Pierrette to sing and act in the opera of *Rose et Colas*, and through her protection the *début* of the unknown actress was so successful that in one representation she earned a suitable portion for a soldier's wife. The merit of this little anecdote of course lies in the management of the details, which, for nature and gracefulness, would do credit to the first names in French literature. Pierrette died young, leaving her husband with two treasures, an only daughter, and a miniature of herself, painted by the Princess de Lamballe. Since then he had lived a life of obscure integrity, and had received all the military honours attainable by a private soldier, but no promotion, which, indeed, he had never much sought, thinking it a greater honour to be a serjeant in the guard than a captain in the line. "How poor," thought M. de Vigny, "are the mad ambitions and discontents of us young officers, compared with the soul of a soldier like this, scrupulous of his honour, and thinking it sullied by the most trifling negligence or breach of discipline; without ambition, vanity, or luxury, always a slave, and always content and proud of his servitude; his dearest recollection being one of gratitude; and believing his destiny to be regulated for his good by an overruling Providence!"

An hour or two after this time the author was awakened from sleep by something like the shock of an earthquake: part of one of the powder magazines had exploded. With difficulty and peril the garrison stopped the spread of mischief. On reaching the seat of the catastrophe, they found the fragments of the body of the old adjutant, who having apparently risen at early dawn for one more examination of the powder, had, by some accident, set it on fire. The King presently arrived to return thanks and distribute rewards: he came, and departed. "I thought," says M. de Vigny, "of the family of the poor adjutant: but I was alone in thinking of them. In general, when princes pass anywhere they pass too quickly."

'La Vie et la Mort du Captaine Renaud, ou, La Canne de Jonc.' is a picture of a more elevated description than either of these two, delineating a character of greater intellectual power, and a loftier moral greatness. The Captain Renaud is a philosopher; one like those of old, who has learnt the wisdom of life from its experiences; has weighed in the balance the greatnesses and littlenesses of the world, and has carried with him from every situation in which he has been placed, and every trial and temptation to which he has been subject, the impressions it was fitted to leave on a thoughtful and sensitive mind. There is no story, no incident, in this life; there is but a noble character, unfolding to us the process of its own formation—not *telling* us, but making us *see* how one circumstance disabused it of false objects of esteem and admiration, how another revealed to it the true. We feel with the young soldier his youthful enthusiasm for Napoleon, and for all of which that name is a symbol; we see this enthusiasm die within him as the truth dawns upon him that this great man is an actor, that the *prestige* with which he overawed the world is in much if not in the largest portion of it the effect of stage-trick, and that a life built upon deception, and directed to essentially selfish ends, is not the ideal he had worshipped. He learns to know a real hero in Collingwood, whose prisoner he is for five years; and never was that most beautiful of military and naval characters drawn in a more loving spirit, or with a nobler appreciation, than in this book. From Collingwood, all his life a martyr to duty—the benignant father and guardian angel of all under his command—who pining for an English home, his children growing up to womanhood without having seen him, lived and died at sea, because his country or his country's institutions could not furnish him a successor;—from him the

126

hero of our author's tale learnt to exchange the paltry admiration of mere power and success, the worship of the vulgar objects of ambition and vanity, for a heartfelt recognition of the greatness of devotion and self-sacrifice. A spirit like that of Collingwood governed and pervaded the remainder of his life. One bitter remembrance he had: it was of a night attack upon a Russian outpost, in which, hardly awakened from sleep, an innocent and beautiful youth, one of the boys of fourteen who sometimes held officers' commissions in the Russian army, fell dead in his grey-haired father's sight, by the unconscious hand of Renaud. He never used sabre more, and was known to the soldiers by carrying ever after a *canne de jonc*, which dropped from the dying hand of the poor boy. Many and solemn were the thoughts on war and the destiny of a soldier, which grew up in him from this passage in his life—nor did it ever cease to haunt his remembrances, and, at times, vex his conscience with misgivings. Unambitious, unostentatious, and therefore unnoticed, he did his duty always and everywhere without reward or distinction, until, in the three days of July 1830, a military point of honor retaining him with his corps on the Royalist side, he received his death-wound by a shot from a poor street-boy—who tended him in tears and remorse in his last moments, and to whom he left by will a provision for his education and maintenance, on condition that he should not become a soldier.

Such is a brief outline of this remarkable book: to which we have felt throughout, and feel still more on looking back, what scanty justice we have done. Among the writings of our day we know not one which breathes a nobler spirit, or in which every detail is conceived and wrought out in a manner more worthy of that spirit. But whoever would know what it is, must read the book itself. No *résumé* can convey any idea of it; the impression it makes is not the sum of the impressions of particular incidents or particular sayings, it is the effect of the tone and color-

127

ing of the whole. We do not seem to be listening to the author, to be receiving a "moral" from any of his stories, or from his characters an "example" prepense; the poem of human life is opened before us, and M. de Vigny does but chaunt from it, in a voice of subdued sadness, a few strains telling of obscure wisdom and unrewarded virtue; of those antique characters which, without self-glorification or hope of being appreciated, "carry out," as he expresses it, "the sentiment of duty to its extremest consequences," and whom he avers, as a matter of personal experience, that he has never met with in any walk of life but the profession of arms.

'Stello' is a work of similar merit to the 'Military Recollections,' though, we think, somewhat inferior. The poet, and his condition—the function he has to perform in the world, and its treatment of him—are the subject of the book. Stello, a young poet, having, it would appear, no personal cause of complaint against the world, but subject to fits of nervous despondency, seeks relief under one of these attacks from a mysterious personage, the *docteur noir*; and discloses to him that in his *ennui* and his thirst for activity and excitement, he has almost determined to fling himself into politics, and sacrifice himself for some one of the parties or forms of government which are struggling with one another in the world. The doctor prescribes to him three stories, exhibiting the fate of the poet under every form of government, and the fruitlessness of his expecting from the world, or from men of the world, aught but negligence or contempt. The stories are of three poets, all of whom the *docteur noir* has seen die, as, in fact, the same person might have been present at all their deaths: under three different governments—an absolute monarchy, a constitutional government, and a democratic revolution. Gilbert, the poet and satirist, called from his poverty Gilbert *sans-culotte*, who died mad in a hospital in Paris, he who wrote in the last days of his life the verses beginning

*128*

> "Au banquet de la vie infortuné convive
> J'apparus un jour, et je meurs"—

Chatterton—

> "the marvellous boy,
> The sleepless soul, who perished in his pride!"—[11]

driven to suicide at eighteen by the anguish of disappointment and neglect; and Andrè Chènier, the elder brother of Chènier the revolutionary poet—whose own poems, published not till many years after his death, were at once hailed by the new school of poetry in France as having anticipated what they have since done, and given the real commencement to the new era: he perished by the guillotine only two days before the fall of Robespierre: on the scaffold he exclaimed, striking his forehead, *"Il y avait pourtant quelque chose là!"* The stories adhere strictly to the spirit of history, though not to the literal facts, and are, as usual, beautifully told, especially the last and most elaborate of them, 'Andrè Chènier.' In this tale we are shown the prison of Saint Lazare during the reign of terror, and the courtesies and gallantries of polished life still blossoming in the foulness of the dungeon and on the brink of the tomb. Madame de St. Aignan, with her reserved and delicate passion for Andrè Chènier, is one of the most graceful of M. de Vigny's creations. We are brought into the presence of Robespierre and Saint Just—who are drawn, not indeed like Catoes and Brutuses, though there have been found in our time Frenchmen not indisposed to take that view of them. But the hatred of exaggeration (that vice of the day) which always characterises M. de Vigny does not desert him here; the terrorist chiefs do not figure in his pages as monsters thirsting for blood, not as hypocrites and imposters with merely the low aims of selfish ambition: either of these representations would

---

[11] Wordsworth's "Resolution and Independence." The same passage is also quoted in the *Biographia Literaria*.

have been false to history. He shows us these men as they were, as such men could not but have been; men distinguished, morally, chiefly by two qualities, entire hardness of heart, and the most overweening and bloated self conceit; for nothing less, assuredly, could lead any man to believe that his individual judgment respecting the public good is a warrant to him for exterminating all who are suspected of forming any other judgment, and for setting up a machine to cut off heads, at sixty or seventy every day, till some unknown futurity be accomplished, some Utopia realized.

The lesson which the *docteur noir* finds in these tragical histories, for the edification of poets, is still that of abnegations: to expect nothing from changes in society or in political institutions; to renounce for ever the idea that the world will, or can be expected to fall at their feet and worship them; to consider themselves, once for all, as martyrs, if they are so, and instead of complaining, to take up their cross and bear it.

This council is so essentially wise and of such deep import, and is so much required everywhere, but above all in France, where the idea that intellect ought to rule the world, an idea in itself true and just, has taken such root that every youth who fancies himself a thinker or an artist thinks he has a right to everything society has to give, and is the victim of ingratitude because he is not loaded with its riches and honours; M. de Vigny has so genuine a feeling of the true greatness of a poet, of the spirit which has dwelt in all poets deserving the name of great—that he may be pardoned for what there is in his picture of a poet's position and destiny in the actual world, somewhat morbid and overcharged, though with a large foundation of universal truth. It is most true that, whether in poetry or in philosophy, a person endowed in any eminent degree with genius—originality—the gift of seeing truths at a greater depth than the world can penetrate, or of feeling deeply and justly things which the world has not yet learnt to feel—that such a person need not hope to be appreciated, to be otherwise than made light of and evil entreated, in virtue of what is greatest in him, his genius. For (except in things which can be reduced to mathematical demonstration or made obvious to sense) which all mankind are prepared to see the *next* minute, it cannot require much genius to perceive in *this*; and all persons of distinguished originality, whether thinkers or artists, are subject to the eternal law, that they must themselves create the taste or the habits of thought by which they will afterwards be appreciated.[12] No great poet or philosopher that ever lived (apart from the accident of a rich patron) could have got either honour or subsistence *as* a poet or a philosopher; but things are not, and have seldom been, so badly ordered in the world, as that he could not get it in any other way. Chatterton, and probably Gilbert, could have earned an honest livelihood, if their inordinate pride would have accepted of it in the common paths of obscure industry. And much as it is to be lamented, for the world's sake more than that of the individual, that they who are equal to the noblest things are not reserved for such, —it is nevertheless true that persons of genius, persons whose superiority is that they can do what others cannot do, can generally also, if they choose, do better than others that which others do, and which others are willing to honour and reward. If they cannot, it is usually from something ill regulated in themselves, something to be cured of which would be for the health even of their own minds; perhaps oftenest because they will not take the pains which less gifted persons are willing to take, although less than half as much would suffice; because the habit of doing with ease things on a large scale, makes them impatient of slow and unattractive toil. It is their own choice

[12] An obscure passage. Mill seems to mean: those things that can be reduced to mathematical expression or demonstrated empirically can be understood quickly even by persons of little intelligence. But the truths of poetry and philosophy are of a different kind and require superior genius to be understood. Moreover, thinkers and artists must be responsible for creating the tastes and capabilities that their works demand.

then. If they wish for worldly honour and profit, let them seek it in the way others do; the struggle indeed is hard, and the attainment uncertain, but not specially so to them; on the contrary, they have advantages over most of their competitors. If they prefer their nobler vocation they have no cause of quarrel with the world because they follow that vocation under the conditions necessarily implied in it. If it were possible that they should have the acclamations of the world, they could not be deserving of them; all they could be doing for the world must be comparatively little; they could not be the great men they fancy themselves.

A story, or a poem, might nevertheless be conceived, which would throw ten fold more light upon the poetic character, and upon the condition of a poet in the world, than any instance, either historical or fictitious, of the world's undervaluing of him. It would exhibit the sufferings of a poet, not from mortified vanity, but from the poetic temperament itself—under arrangements of society made by and for harder natures, and in a world which its Creator himself did not intend to be a place of contentment or peace for any but the unsensitive. That M. de Vigny could conceive such a subject in the spirit in which it should be conceived, is clear from the signs by which his Stello recognizes himself as a poet. "Because there is in nature no beauty, nor grandeur, nor harmony, which does not cause in me a prophetic thrill, which does not fill me with a deep emotion and swell my eyelids with tears divine and inexplicable. Because of the infinite pity I feel for mankind, my companions in suffering and the eager desire I feel to hold out my hand to them and raise them incessantly by words of commiseration and of love. Because I feel in my inmost being an invisible and undefinable power which resembles a presentiment of the future, and a revelation of the mysterious causes of the present:" a presentiment which is not always imaginary, but often the instinctive insight of a sensitive nature, which from its finer texture vibrates to impressions so evanescent as to be unfelt by others, and, by that faculty as by an additional sense, is apprised it cannot tell how, of things without, which escape the cognizance of the less delicately organized.

These *are* the tests, or some of the tests, of a poetic nature; and it must be evident that to such, even when supported by a positive religious faith, and that a cheerful one, this life is naturally, or at least may easily be, a vale of tears; a place in which there is no rest. The poet who would speak of such, must do it in the spirit of those beautiful lines of Shelley—himself the most perfect type of that which he described:

> "High, spirit-winged heart, who dost for ever
> Beat thy unfeeling bars with vain endeavour,
> Till those bright plumes of thought, in which arrayed
> It over-soared this low and worldly shade
> Lie shattered, and thy panting, wounded breast
> Stains with dear blood its unmaternal nest!
> I weep vain tears: blood would less bitter be
> Yet poured forth gladlier, could it profit thee."[13]

The remainder of M. de Vigny's works are plays and poems. The plays are 'Le More de Venise,' a well-executed and very close translation of Othello; 'La Maréchale d'Ancre,' from the same period of history as Cinq-Mars; and 'Chatterton,' the story in Stello, with the characters more developed, the outline more filled up. Without disparagement to these works, we think the narrative style more suitable than the dramatic to the quality of M. de Vigny's genius. If we had not read these plays, we should not have known how much of the impressiveness of his other writings comes from his own *presence* in them (if the expression may be allowed), animating and harmonizing the picture, by blending with it natural tints the colouring of his own feelings and character.

Of the poems much were to be said, if a foreigner could be

[13] "Epipsychidion."

considered altogether a competent judge of them. For our own part we confess that, of the admirable poetry which abounds in French literature, that part is most poetry to us which is written in prose.[14] In regard to verse-writing we would even exceed the severity of Horace's precept against mediocrity; we hold, that nothing should be written in verse which is not exquisite. In prose, anything may be said which is worth saying at all; in verse, only what is worth saying better than prose can say it. The gems alone of thought and fancy, are worth setting with so finished and elaborate a workmanship; and even of them, those only whose effect is heightened by it: which takes place under two conditions; and in one or other of these two, if we are not mistaken, must be found the origin and justification of all composition in verse. A thought or feeling requires verse for its adequate expression, when in order that it may dart into the soul with the speed of a lightning-flash, the ideas or images that are to convey it require to be pressed closer together than is compatible with the rigid grammatical construction of prose: this the inversions and elisions of verse, afford the means of accomplishing. One recommendation of verse, therefore is, that it affords a language more *condensed* than prose. The other, is derived from one of the natural laws of the human mind in the utterance of its thoughts impregnated with its feelings. All emotion which had taken possession of the whole being—which flows unresistedly, and therefore equably—instinctively seeks a language that flows equably like itself; and must either find it, or be conscious of an unsatisfied want, which even impedes and prematurely stops the flow of the feeling. Hence, ever since man has been man, all deep and sustained feeling has tended to express itself in rhythmical language; and the deeper the feeling, the more characteristic and decided the rhythm: provided

[14] Mill, as he goes on to explain, means poetry in the nongeneric sense. These remarks extend the definitions set forth in the 1833 essays on poetry. For an interesting defense of these ideas see Mill's letters to George Henry Lewes: *Mill, The Earlier Letters*, ed. Mineka, 463–64, 466.

always the feeling be sustained as well as deep; for, a *fit* of passion has no natural connexion with verse or music, a *mood* of passion has the strongest. No one who does not hold this distinction in view, will comprehend the importance which the Greek lawgivers and philosophers attached to music, and which appears inexplicable till we understand how perpetual an aim of their polity it was to subdue *fits* of passion, and to sustain and reinforce *moods* of it*.[15] This view of the origin of rhythmic utterance in general, and verse in particular, naturally demands *short* poems, it being impossible that a feeling so intense as to require a more rhythmical cadence than that of eloquent prose, should sustain itself at its highest elevation for long together:[16] and we are persuaded that, except in the ages when the absence of written books occasioned all things to be thrown into verse for facility of memory, or in those other ages in which writing in verse may happen to be a *fashion*, a long poem will always be felt to be something unnatural and hollow; something which it requires the genius of a Homer, a Dante, or a Milton, to induce posterity to read, or at least to read through.

Verse, then, being only allowable where prose would be inadequate and the inadequacy of prose arising either from its not being sufficiently condensed, or from its not having cadence enough to express sustained passion, which is never

---

* Milton understood this:—

> "The dorian mood
> Of flutes and soft recorders; such as raised
> To height of noblest temper heroes old
> Arming to battle; and, *instead of rage*,
> *Deliberate valour breathed*, firm and unmoved
> With dread of death, to flight or foul retreat:
> Nor wanting power to mitigate and swage,
> With solemn touches, troubled thoughts, and chase
> Anguish, and doubt, and fear, and sorrow and pain,
> From mortal or immortal minds."
>
> [*Paradise Lost*, I, 550; Mill's note.]

[15] *Paradise Lost*, I, 550.

[16] Another idea usually associated with Coleridge: see *Biographia*, II: 11; also chapter XIV *passim*.

long-winded—it follows, that if prolix writing is vulgarly called *prosy* writing, a very true feeling of the distinction between verse and prose shows itself in the vulgarism; and that the one unpardonable sin in a versified composition, next to the absence of meaning, and of true meaning, is diffuseness. From this sin it will be impossible to exculpate M. Alfred de Vigny. His poems, graceful and often fanciful though they be, are, to us, marred by their diffuseness.

Of the more considerable among them, that which most resembles what, in our conception, a poem in verse ought to be, is 'Moise.' The theme is still the sufferings of the man of genius, the inspired man, the intellectual ruler and seer; not however this time, the great man persecuted by the world, but the great man honoured by it, and in his natural place at the helm of it, the man on whom all rely, whom all reverence— Moses on Pisgah, Moses the appointed of God, the judge, captain, and hierarch of the chosen race—crying to God, in anguish of spirit for deliverance and rest; that the cares and toils, the weariness and solitariness of heart, of him who is lifted altogether above his brethren, be no longer imposed upon him—that the Almighty may withdraw his gifts, and suffer him to sleep the sleep of common humanity. His cry is heard; when the clouds disperse, which veiled the summit of the mountain from the Israelites waiting in prayer and prostration at its foot, Moses is no more seen: and now, "marching towards the promised land, Joshua advanced, pale and pensive of mien; for he was already the chosen of the Omnipotent."

The longest of the poems is 'Eloa; or the Sister of the Angels;' a story of a bright being, created from a tear of the Redeemer, and who falls, tempted by pity for the Spirit of Darkness. The idea is fine, and the details graceful, a word we have often occasion to use in speaking of M. de Vigny: but this and most of his other poems are written in the heroic verse, that is to say, he has aggravated the imperfections, for his purpose, of the most prosaic language in Europe, by choosing to write in its most prosaic metre. The absence of prosody, of long and short or accented and unaccented syllables, renders the French language essentially unmusical; while—the unbending structure of its sentence, of which there is essentially but one type for verse and prose, almost precluding inversions and elisions—all the screws and pegs of the prose sentence are retained to encumber the verse. If it is to be raised at all above prose, variety of rhythm must be sought in variety of versification; there is no room for it in the monotonous structure of the heroic metre. Where is it that Racine, always an admirable writer, appears to us more than an admirable *prose* writer? In his irregular metres—in the chorusses of Esther and of Athalie. It is not wonderful then if the same may be said of M. de Vigny. We shall conclude with the following beautiful little poem, one of the few which he has produced in the style and measure of lyric verse:—

> "Viens sur la mer, jeune fille,
>    Sois sans effroi;
> Viens sans trésor, sans famille,
>    Seule avec moi.
> Mon bateau sur les eaux brille,
>    Voi ses mâts, voi
> Ses pavillons et sa quille.
> Ce n'est rien qu'une coquille,
>    Mais j'y suis roi.
>
> Pour l'esclave on fit la terre,
>    O ma beauté!
> Mais pour l'homme libre, austère,
>    L'immensité.
>    Les flots savent un mystère
>    De volupté;
> Leur soupir involuntaire
> Veut dire: amour solitaire,
>    Et liberté."

A.

# Bibliography

The following is a brief selection of books and articles concerned with aspects of Mill's literary theory.

Abrams, M. H. *The Mirror and the Lamp*. New York, 1953.

Alexander, Edward. *Matthew Arnold and John Stuart Mill*. New York, 1965.

————. "Mill's Theory of Culture; the Wedding of Literature and Democracy." *University of Toronto Quarterly* XXXV (1965): 75–88.

Hainds, John Robert. "John Stuart Mill's *Examiner* articles on Art." *Journal of the History of Ideas* XI (1950): 215–34.

Myoshi, Masao. "Mill and 'Pauline': The Myth and Some Facts." *Victorian Studies* IX (1965): 154–63.

Petersen, William S., and Standley, Frederick. "The J. S. Mill Marginalia in Robert Browning's *Pauline*: a History and Transcription." *Papers of the Bibliographic Society of America* LXVI (1972): 135–70.

Preyer, Robert. "The Utilitarian Poetics; John Stuart Mill." *University of Kansas City Review* XIX (1952): 131–36.

Robson, John M. "Harriet Taylor and John Stuart Mill: Artist and Scientist." *Queen's Quarterly* LXXIII (1966): 167–86.

————. *The Improvement of Mankind: the Social and Political Thought of John Stuart Mill*. Toronto, 1968.

————. "J. S. Mill's Theory of Poetry." *University of Toronto Quarterly* XXIX (1960): 420–38.

Sharpless, F. Parvin. *The Literary Criticism of John Stuart Mill*. The Hague, 1967.

————. "William Johnson Fox and Mill's Essays on Poetry." *Victorian Newsletter* 27 (1965): 18–21.

The following is a chronological selection of Mill's other writings on poetry, poetic process, and the relation of art to society. Irregularities in the numbering of volumes is caused by changes in ownership during the period of Mill's contributions. In 1835, dissatisfied with the editorial policies of the *Westminster Review*, Mill began a competing publication called the *London Review*. The next year, aided by funds from Sir William Molesworth, Mill purchased the *Westminster* and combined it with the *London Review*, calling it the *London and Westminster Review*. In 1840, Mill gave up the proprietorship, and the old title was reinstated.

"On Genius." *Monthly Repository* VI (1832): 649–59.

"De Tocqueville on Democracy in America." *London Review* II (*Westminster Review* XXXI) (1835): 85–129.

"Civilization—Signs of the Times." *London and Westminster Review* XXV (1836): 1–28.

"The French Revolution." *London and Westminster Review* XXVII (1837): 17–53 [on Carlyle's history].

"Aphorisms—Thoughts in the Cloister and the Crowd." *London and Westminster Review* XXVI (1837): 348–57.

"Milne's Poems of Many Years." *London and Westminster Review* XXIX (1838): 308–20.

"Bentham." *London and Westminster Review* XXIX (1838): 467–506.

"Coleridge." *London and Westminster Review* XXXIII (1840): 257–302.

"Lays of Ancient Rome." *Westminster Review* XXXIX (1843): 105–13 [Macaulay's *Lays of Ancient Rome*].

"Inaugural Address delivered to the University of St. Andrew's." London, 1867.

*Analysis of the Phenomena of the Human Mind*, by James Mill. J. S. Mill, ed. 2 vols. London, 1869 [extensive notes by John Stuart Mill].

*Three Essays on Religion: Nature, The Utility of Religion, and Theism*. London, 1874.

# Index

Architecture, "poetry" of, 20–21
Associationalist psychology. *See* Utilitarianism, associationalist psychology in

Bain, Alexander, viii
Balzac, Honore de: historical accuracy in, 116, 117; as a Royalist writer, 85
Beautiful, the, 115–16
Beethoven: *Fidelio*, 15; overture to *Egmont*, 16
Bentham, Jeremy, ix, x
*Blackwood's Magazine*, 46–47
Byron, George Gordon: as a political poet, 79, 80 n; style of, 89

Carlyle, Thomas: as a historical writer, 18 n; interest of, in Hellenism, 19 n; his opinion of Mill, vii, 28–29
Chateaubriand, Francois René, vicomte de, 118
Chatterton, Thomas: in de Vigny's work, 129; as an unappreciated poet, 131
Claude Lorrain (painter), 20
Coleridge, Samuel Taylor: *Biographia Literaria*, 30 n, 135 n;

cited by Mill, 29, 61, 69 n; as a philosopher-poet, 42
Conservative poet, the. *See* Politics
Croker, John Wilson, 46–47

Dante, 135
David, Jacques-Louis, 19, 61 n
de Tocqueville, Alexis. *See* Tocqueville, Alexis de
de Vigny, Alfred Victor. *See* Vigny, Alfred Victor de
*Dissertations and Discussions* (Mill), xix
Dumas, Alexandre, 116

Earnestness in art, 115–16
Eliot, T. S., 12 n
Elliott, Ebenezer, 11
Emotion. *See* Feeling
Englishmen, national character of, 79
Experientialist metaphysics, Mill's commitment to, xiv–xvii, 75–76

Fancy, 33, 70
Feeling: in architecture, 20–21; in *Cinq-Mars*, 117; combined with thought, 41–43, 46, 68–70; con-

*141*

Composition by Graphic Composition, Inc., of Athens, Georgia.
Printed offset by Thomson-Shore, Inc., of Ann Arbor, Michigan, on
Warren's University Text. This acid-free paper, noted for its longevity,
has been watermarked with the University of South Carolina Press colophon.
Designed by Larry Hirst.